T0107181

The **10**

Qualities *of* Influential People

The # 10

Qualities *of* Influential People

HOW TO INSPIRE YOURSELF
AND OTHERS TO *GREATNESS*

BRIAN TRACY

MEDIA

Published 2022 by Gildan Media LLC
aka G&D Media
www.GandDmedia.com

Copyright © 2022 by Brian Tracy

An earlier version of the this book was sold under the title *The Science of Influence*. This current version has been retitled, reorganized and expanded for an improved customer experience.

No part of this book may be used, reproduced or transmitted in any manner whatsoever, by any means (electronic, photocopying, recording, or otherwise), without the prior written permission of the author, except in the case of brief quotations embodied in critical articles and reviews. No liability is assumed with respect to the use of the information contained within. Although every precaution has been taken, the author and publisher assume no liability for errors or omissions. Neither is any liability assumed for damages resulting from the use of the information contained herein.

First Edition: 2022

Cover design by Tom McKeveny

Interior design by Meghan Day Healey of Story Horse, LLC.

Library of Congress Cataloging-in-Publication Data is available upon request

ISBN: 978-1-7225-0542-4

10 9 8 7 6 5 4 3 2 1

Contents

Foreword

Influence is one of the most powerful skills you can develop. Without it, all other aspects of human relations are ineffective at best and failures at worst.

If you attempt to communicate your business idea to an investor but lack the skill of influence, your idea will fall flat, and you will not generate the venture capital that you need.

If you want your children to adopt your deepest moral values but lack the skill of influence, your efforts will pale in comparison to the ploys of social media and peer pressure.

If you want to convince your spouse that they need to take their health seriously but lack the skill of influence, they may ultimately get the bad news at the doctor's office when it is too late.

Maybe you're trying to break an addiction to caffeine or web surfing. If you lack the skill of influence, you'll be unable to convince yourself that delaying your gratification and establishing an empowering new habit is even worth it.

Influence is like the combination on a strong titanium lock. Imagine that the ability to communicate is the spinning of that lock, which gives you access to the mind. Bad communication, through endless talking, inattentive listening, or overbearing manners, is like spinning the numbers on the lock randomly. Developing the basic skills of influence is like knowing the exact combination to that lock, which gives you access to the minds and hearts of others—or yourself.

That's what you'll learn in this book: the specific numbers to the highly guarded combination that will enable you to produce incredible results—happier personal relationships, more sales, more profitable partnerships, and more power to commit yourself to your most important goals.

Ideas about influence started back in ancient times, continued through the Renaissance, and progressed through the twentieth century with landmark publications like Dale Carnegie's *How to Win Friends and Influence People*. Insights into this subject continue to advance. This book follows in that tradition, updating time-honored truths with new discoveries in psychology, neuroscience, and business theory.

This book will open the lock of influence for you. You will learn the top ten qualities of influential people. You'll learn the key principles of influence. You'll also learn how to cultivate these qualities in yourself and how to use them in different areas of life—in sales, with your coworkers, with your family. You will rapidly move from theory to fact.

When you're finished with this book, you'll know—and will have absorbed—the ten top qualities of influential people. You'll know how to apply them everywhere in your life. These skills will move you towards the goals that you wish for in your deepest heart and will bring you the satisfaction you want.

Introduction

The Many Faces of Influence

One of the best definitions of influence that I've heard recently is *moving*. *Moving*, in this sense, means taking a person from one way of thinking to another.

If you look back 6,000 years, you will see that human beings have one primary motivation: improvement. All attempts to sell and all attempts to buy are intended to improve one's condition in some way.

We call this the ABC theory of motivation. "A" stands for *antecedents*, which is where you are before you are influenced; "B" are the *behaviors* that you take as a result of influence; "C" are the *consequences*. The formula

---

The ABC Theory of Motivation

A stands for Antecedents

B stands for Behaviors

C stands for Consequences

---

is that 15 percent of your actions are determined by antecedents—previous events—and 85 percent of your motivation to move, to change, comes from the anticipated consequences.

What, then, is the starting point for gaining access to this unused treasure? The first step is to realize that it is there. You have more potential than you can use in a hundred lifetimes. Millions of people all over the world have gone from rags to riches, become millionaires and billionaires, in a single lifetime. What they have done, you can do as well. I will show you what other people, starting with nothing, did that transformed their lives. It turned the switch and opened the door. Even an average person who follows certain steps in a systematic and orderly way will become influential.

My late friend Og Mandino, author of *The Greatest Salesman in the World*, once said to me, "Brian, there are no secrets of success. There are simple rules and principles that have been discovered and rediscovered throughout all of human history. All you have to do is learn and practice them, and you'll get the same results as the most successful companies."

Surprise, surprise—this process works. To influence people, you need to take a certain series of steps. If you do this in the right way, people will be open to your influence. In fact, they will want to be influenced by you; they will seek your guidance and direction. You'll get results beyond any you've ever thought possible.

The words *influence* and *persuasion* are often treated as if they're synonymous, but I think they are different. You can influence people without trying to persuade them of anything—just by being a particular kind of person. One example is the role model: someone whom other people observe and imitate. People who believe that you are a person of character, clarity, and conviction will be much more influenced by you than if they believe otherwise.

Parents are responsible for 40 to 50 percent of a child's habits. Children are greatly influenced, not just by their parents' efforts at persuasion, but also by their behavior. Your children will behave toward people in their world the way you behave toward people in your world—especially your spouse. Someone once said, "The kindest thing that a man can do for his children is to love their mother."

My wife and I understood these principles when we got married. My children have always seen my wife and me show each other a high level of respect. All of them in turn have grown up to marry people that they respected and who respected them, and they all treat these spouses and children the same way. They also treat other people well and expect to be treated well in return.

In his book *In Search of Excellence*, Tom Peters emphasized that a parent can change a child's psychological dynamic just by being an example. Children may ignore what you say, but they watch everything that you do, which they absorb through the skin. If you treat your children with respect, they will treat others the same way and will expect to be treated with respect too. As a parental role model, you have tremendous influence.

Persuasion, on the other hand, is convincing a person to behave in a way they would not have otherwise behaved. Because people do things for their own reasons, not for yours, your goal is to find out what they want and to show them the fastest and simplest way to get it.

As we can see, sometimes influence has little to do with words at all. You don't say anything: you use the law of indirect effort. If you want to impress a person, the fastest way is to be impressed by them. If you want a person to like you, the fastest way is for you to like them. The more you can be impressed by someone and find them

---

Use the Law of Indirect Effort. If you want to impress a person, the fastest way is to be impressed by them.

"You can easily judge the character of a man by how he
treats those who can do nothing for him."
—Johann Wolfgang von Goethe

---

valuable and important, the more they start to think of
you as an interesting and charismatic person.

This all goes back to the basic rule: who is everyone's
favorite person? Themselves. Whom do people think
about 99 percent of the time? Themselves. A person who's
sitting with a toothache can be surrounded by a crowd,
but he's thinking more about that toothache than about
everybody around him, the news of the day, or what's on
television. His sore tooth preoccupies 99 percent of his
mental activity.

No one can have any influence over you unless you
want something from them, something that you want
them to do for you, or something that you want them *not*
to do to you. If a person cannot change your life in any
way, they have very little influence over you. Indeed the
great German poet and philosopher Johann Wolfgang
von Goethe said, "You can easily judge the character of a
man by how he treats those who can do nothing for him."

Imagine walking down the street. There's a home-
less person who's obviously not in their right mind, and
they're shouting at you and everybody else as they walk
along. This person has no influence over you, because

there's nothing they can do to you or for you; they can't help you or hurt you in any way.

By contrast, someone at a higher level in your organization can do a great deal to hurt or help you. One form of power in an organization is *position power*. A person with position power can have tremendous influence over us because they can do something to us or for us, or stop something being done to or for us.

That's why subordinates suck up to a new boss. The boss arrives on Monday morning; people get in early, and they're happy to see the boss. They bring the boss a cup of coffee and ask, "How can I help you? What can I do for you? Is there anything that you need?" Or they immediately try to position themselves: "I am the top salesman in this company, my sales are higher than anyone else's, so I'm usually the critical factor in making sales quota in this office. I'm really looking forward to working with you."

You want to establish yourself with the boss, because bosses have power—they can hand out offices; they can give you the right to wear different clothes; they can grant time off. Their position power is very strong. You may never have met or spoken to this person before, but they have influence over you because of their position. With that comes the power to do things for you or against you, to help you or to hurt you.

Human beings are focused on expediency. The deepest level of expediency is, first of all, safety. You want to

> ## Two types of organizational power
>
> 1. Position power—a form of power that accrues to you as a result of your level in the organization. Such power can be given and taken away by others.
> 2. Ascribed power—a form of power that accrues to you as a result of how good you are at what you do. Such power cannot be taken away by others—you carry it with you.

be safe, especially in your job. The second level is security. When I've been brought in as the president of a company (as I have a number of times), everybody immediately recognizes that I now control who sits in what office, who has what job, who goes to a meeting, and who has what position. People are vying for my favor because I can help or hurt them in some way.

We had a striking illustration of position power several years ago in the United States. Before the presidential election of 2016, millions of people were completely convinced that the man who was eventually elected president was going to lose in a landslide. Influencers were making plans and passing out the power that they thought they would have when the new presidential dynamic took place after November 8.

The next day, the game had changed completely; the whole calculation was different. Now, completely unexpectedly, a new person was about to become the president of the United States.

Everybody was shocked. The influence and persuasion dynamics of the entire country, and of the world, were overturned. People were reeling and backing up: those who had been stridently taking one position were now stridently taking another. Power suddenly shifted. In a matter of hours, as people watched the electoral map, they realized that the dreams, fantasies, hopes, and wishes of 160 million members of the electorate had suddenly changed forever. It can happen very quickly.

Some corporations get into trouble because the chief executive officer has made bad decisions, which have led to large losses. The board of directors steps in and appoints a new president, who then appoints new subordinates. Suddenly all the old powers-that-be are out the door. The whole company is different, it's being run by a different person, and the new person's people are running everything. Yesterday you were a big player with an important position, a large office, and a large staff, and today you're nothing. Your ability to influence is gone overnight because you can no longer do something for or against someone.

My friend Dan Kennedy, who is a very smart marketing expert, said, "Be careful whom you step on as you climb the ladder of success, because they're going to be waiting for you with drawn daggers when you come back down." Here's another wonderful one-liner from Dan: "In life, friends come and go, but enemies accumulate."

Another type of power in organizations is called *ascribed power*. This is where you are recognized as being very good at what you do. A person who has this reputation is usually the one who attracts and holds on to the most power. Unlike position power, which is externally granted and can be taken away, it's something that you're known for being: you carry it with you.

Let's talk specifically about the principles involved in making the skill of influence a habitual way of thinking and acting. Robert Cialdini's book *Influence*, which is a classic, details some of these.

The first is the *law of reciprocity*. If you do something to help or hurt me, I feel a need to reciprocate. If you do something nice for me, I want to do something nice back. If you pay for lunch, I want to pay for lunch the next time; sometimes I want to pay for dinner. In other situations, there is no actual degree of reciprocity in that one person will do much more than the other.

Whenever you do nice things for others, you predispose them to doing nice things for you. Offering to lend a person your lawnmower or your car, or offering to pick up something or take them somewhere, will create a desire

---

Four Principles to Develop
The Skill of Influence

1. The Law of Reciprocity
2. Commitment and Consistency
3. Social proof
4. Authority

---

in them to reciprocate: they feel they owe you one. Since about 95 percent of human beings dislike feeling under obligation to someone else, they will look for ways to pay you back.

That's why the smartest people are always looking for ways to do favors for others. Recently I watched the complete eight-hour series of *The Godfather*. It showed a man who came over as an immigrant, worked in an Italian neighborhood, and did favors for people. He helped a grandmother find a home for her cat and dog and other little things like that around the neighborhood. Then he would go back and say, "I helped you here; would you help me there?" They would help him back. Pretty soon he had developed a network of favors, and by the time he was finished, he controlled half of the judges in New York. He had done something nice for their daughters when they got married, or had helped with a piece of legislation, a bill, or some financial support. He had all these people in his pockets because he would say, "I'll do you this favor, and perhaps sometime in the future I will ask you for a favor, and you will help me as well." This reciprocity made him the most powerful man in New York.

Whenever you can do something nice for a person, do it. Offer to help them out: offer to pick up something from the store, offer the use of your car or house or even a temporary financial loan. These things predispose them to pay you back when the time comes. According to studies of power, the most influential people have helped others, even if they have no direct control over them. Their beneficiaries are predisposed to help them in turn.

There is also the *hopes and dreams* trigger. You help others achieve their hopes and dreams.

I once knew a woman who had a friend in college. The friend needed help for an exam, and she helped her friend pass it. Later the first woman's daughter was in college, but she was stuck in a campus 500 miles from the capital. She wanted to be transferred to the main campus. The administration told her, "No, there's no way we can do it."

The woman called her friend and told her she was having these problems. The friend said, "I know somebody who knows somebody." They went to someone in the registrar's office who shuffled some papers around and got the daughter transferred from the distant campus to the main campus.

Help people with their hopes and dreams, and they'll help with yours.

Another method of psychological influence is *commitment and consistency*. People may start off with little or no commitment to a cause, but gradually they can develop one. One example is a political campaign. A campaigner goes up and down the street and asks, "Would you put a billboard on your lawn for this candidate?"

The homeowner says, "No, I don't know the candidate, and the sign would clutter up my yard."

"OK, well, would you put up just a little decal that says 'Support Joe for City Council'?"

"Sure."

Two weeks later, the campaigner comes back and says, "The campaign's going really well. Would you put up a little bigger sign that says 'Support Joe'?"

"Yes."

In two weeks, the campaigner comes back again and says, "Boy, you're really making a difference here. You're a good citizen, you're helping people in the community, you're making your position known. Would you put up a billboard?"

"Absolutely."

The homeowner's first reaction was flat-out refusal. After six weeks, he has a billboard on his lawn supporting Joe. Over time, with approval, reaffirmation, and repeated requests, he's made a huge commitment. That's

"Help people with their hopes and dreams,
and they'll help with yours."
—Brian Tracy

why you can start off asking people for a small contribution, and then they'll give you a bigger contribution, and then a bigger one.

Another powerful method of influence is *social proof*: people who are initially opposed to a course of action will change their minds 180 degrees if they find out that someone they know and respect is doing it. This a very powerful way of influencing people.

You say, for example, "Would you support this particular cause?"

The person says, "No. I have no interest in it."

"Did you know that your best friend on the next block has already supported and contributed to this cause? He said that you're such a good person that you'd probably support it as well."

"Oh, my best friend, the guy I went to school with—if he said he's supporting it, then I'll support it." You have a 180-degree turn because of somebody the person knows.

This is why many companies use well-known sports figures to advertise their products: people who respect the figure will feel that the product is a good one. Michael Jordan has generated more than a billion dollars in sales by appearing on a basketball court in a commercial. He doesn't speak; he bounces the ball, then shoots it through a hoop. The commercial says, "Michael Jordan. Nike shoes. Just do it."

Another powerful form of influence is *authority*. For example, when a doctor recommends a medication, you are much more likely to trust or at least try it.

The influence of authority can take unusual forms. Say there's a man who is gravely ill, convinced he's going to die. He has given up; he no longer has the will to resist. Since about 50 percent of the efficacy of modern medicine is through the placebo effect, if you believe you're going to die, you're probably correct.

The doctor tells the patient, "Good news! The foremost authority on your medical condition in the country is visiting our hospital today, and he's agreed to see you, talk to you, and give us his analysis of your condition."

The expert comes in, but he's actually an actor dressed up like a doctor, with a white smock, a stethoscope, and a chart. He pretends to carry out a full examination and takes the real doctor outside the room. They're gone for about five or ten minutes, then the real doctor comes back in and says, "Wow, have we ever got some great news! This doctor said that you have just reached the turning point in your ailment—and he's never wrong. From this moment onward, you're going to get better and better. Within a couple of weeks, you're going to be out of the hospital and back to normal." After that, the patient starts to recover.

Influence is so powerful that, under certain circumstances, it can achieve more remarkable results than modern medicine.

The Ten Qualities of Influential People

1. Goals
2. Integrity
3. Attitude
4. Sincerity
5. Being well-informed
6. Preparation
7. Loving People
8. Communication
9. Good manners
10. Perseverance

1

The First Quality: Goals

In the introduction, I've given an overview of some of the most important principles of influence. Let's now explore what influential people are like. While they come from all income levels, races, genders, backgrounds, and personality styles, they share ten unique qualities.

Possibly the most important is *goal orientation*. Influential people are goal-oriented: you cannot imagine a leader without goals.

Influential people come from all income levels,
races, genders, backgrounds and personality styles;
but they are all goal-oriented.

As of late 2021, there were about 2,755 billionaires in the world. Astonishingly, there are an estimated 20 million millionaires worldwide. In both of these categories, about 87 percent are self-made.

Researchers asked these successful individuals, "Why are you so wealthy? How were you able to make so much money in such a short time?"

The answers were remarkably similar. In the first place, these people said, "I had a clear goal of being financially independent." They had clear goals and written plans, and they worked very hard—up to sixteen hours a day, five to six days a week—usually for five to seven years.

These individuals also said, "I was willing to try everything." That's another quality of self-made entrepreneurial successes: they will try many different things. If one thing doesn't work, they'll try something else. If that doesn't work, they'll try something else again.

Another characteristic of wealthy individuals who are self-made is that they are willing to take risks. Every so often you have to go all in, like in Texas Hold'em poker, because you have an opportunity with a big upside and a big downside.

The ability to set goals is connected to maturity. Recent research shows that the human brain does not fully develop until the age of twenty-five. At that point, it begins to think in the long term. Before then, the brain is short-term-oriented—immediate gratification, short-term pleasure. The future is fuzzy, vague, unimportant. Only after the age of twenty-five to twenty-seven do people start to set long-term goals.

I myself was twenty-four or twenty-five when I discovered goals, and I thought I'd died and gone to heaven. I couldn't believe how powerful goals are. It was like driving across country in a strange land and never being able to find your way anywhere, and then discovering and learning how to use road maps. Once I learned to use goals, I realized that you could make much more progress much faster, and more easily and predictably.

When I discovered goals, I was sleeping on the floor of a small one-room apartment, which I shared with someone else. I read an article in an old magazine that said, "If you want to be successful, you have to have goals." I took a scrap of paper and wrote down ten goals.

Although I lost the paper and the article, I remember the goals, because I wrote down ridiculous ones. Ten days later, I had achieved all of them.

At that time, I was earning $100 a month and just staying alive, so I wrote down a goal to earn $1,000 a month. Because I found a new way to sell, open calls, and close sales, I began to earn that amount. At that point, I was the top salesman in the company, so they made me the manager and had me train everybody else.

Suddenly, my whole life began to change. I became excited about goals, so I got a pad and I began to write them down, as well as lists of things that I could do to achieve them. Then I began to review the lists and do something to achieve my goals each day.

Inspirational speaker Earl Nightingale said that happiness is the progressive realization of a worthy ideal or goal. Whenever you feel yourself moving step by step towards something that's important to you, you feel happier, you have more energy, and you're more creative, positive, and influential. As you work and achieve one goal, you start to achieve others as well. As you do, you get more energy and confidence, which causes you to want to set other goals. When you accomplish them, you feel even happier.

Happy people are far more influential than negative people, so a wonderful way to be more influential is to have clear goals. A person who knows what they want, is working toward it every day, and has a feeling of progress is far more impressive and influential than someone who's just hanging around. When you have goals, you come into the office, your day is planned, and you're ready to go to work. It makes a big difference.

Today I'm the best-selling author in at least twenty-two languages on how to set and achieve goals. Countless people from all over the world tell me that my audios, videos, and books on goal setting have made them rich.

"Happiness is the progressive realization of a
worthy ideal or goal." —Earl Nightingale

They'd been drifting for years until they read the book
or listened to the audio. They followed the instructions
and transformed their lives. Their incomes went up, they
moved to nicer homes, and they lost weight.

One of the fastest ways to build self-confidence is to
make a list of ten goals that you'd like to achieve in the
next year. Then ask yourself, "Which one goal, if I were
to achieve it, would have the greatest positive impact on
my life?"

How to Accomplish Goals

1. Write down a list of ten goals.
2. Go through the list and determine which is most important.
3. Write down this goal on another piece of paper.
4. Write down ten activities that will help you attain this goal.
5. Pick out the single most important activity that will help you reach your goal.
6. Carry out that activity.
7. Repeat as needed.

Go over the list and pick one goal. Imagine that that goal is guaranteed to be achieved. Write it on a separate piece of paper, along with the things you can do to accomplish it. Then ask, "Of all the things I can do to attain that goal, which one would be the most helpful?"

Now you have your most important goal and your most important activity. You take action on your most important activity, and you work on it every single day. This is a profound life changer. If you follow these instructions, you'll notice the difference almost instantly. As you work on your goal, you start to attract into your life people, circumstances, ideas, and energy to help move you toward it.

I remember reading a book by the Russian metaphysician P. D. Ouspensky many years ago. It consisted of a series of questions from students and his answers. One student asked, "What should I do in this particular situation? There are so many details, and I'm so confused."

"What is your aim?" Ouspensky asked.

"What do you mean?"

"What is your aim? What is your ultimate goal? What do you ultimately want to accomplish in this situation, and where do you want to end up?"

"I don't know. I'm not clear about that."

"Then I cannot give you any guidance on what your behavior should be. Until you are clear about your aim, it's impossible to determine the ideal behavior for the moment. You have to be clear about your aim. Your activity then should be anything that moves you in the direction of that aim."

There's a story about a traveler who was hiking along a path in ancient Greece. He came across an old man clothed in a white robe, who was sitting on a stone. He said to the old man, "Excuse me. I've lost my way, and I wonder if you can tell me how to get to Mount Olympus."

The old man, who turned out to be the philosopher Socrates, said, "If you really want to get to Mount Olympus, it's very simple. Just make sure that every step you take is in that direction."

Do you want to double your productivity and income? Imagine that you have two types of activities. We'll call them activities number one and number two. Number one activities move you toward the goals that you want to accomplish. Number two activities do not move you toward your goals, or, even worse, move you away from your goals.

Here's how you can double your productivity, performance, and income: do only number one activities, and refuse to do number two activities. It's as simple as that.

Before you do anything, ask yourself, "Is this activity moving me towards something that I really want to

---

Before you do anything, ask yourself:
"Is this activity moving me closer towards something I
really want to accomplish, or is it just a distraction?"

---

accomplish, or is it just a distraction?" If this activity is not moving you toward any of your goals, then simply don't do it and do something that is.

If you follow this procedure on a regular basis, in about three days you'll be spending your time on things that are moving you toward your most important goals in health, wealth, personal success, business, and family life. You'll also start doing fewer and fewer of the other things. As long as you focus on number one activities, you're doing good things with your life.

Number two activities give you no pleasure at all. They have no emotional food value. You can do them all day—playing with your email, checking your phone, making calls, talking to your friends, reading the paper—but you get zero nutrition from them. At the end of the day, you're dissatisfied and stressed. You feel you've made no progress at all, and you're angry with yourself.

When you see yourself making progress on things that are important to you, you feel happy all the time. When you feel happy, you have more energy. When you have more energy, you're more creative. When you're more creative, you want to do more of the things that are moving you closer to what is important to you. It's a very simple technique for doubling your income, and it's a very good way of guiding your whole life.

This is one of the great success principles: if you want to have a fabulous life, just make sure that everything that you do is consistent with where you want to end up later in life.

A great deal of work has been done over the last twenty-five years on strategic planning. It has shown that knowing where you want to be five years from now dramatically improves short-term decision making. If you know exactly where you want to be in five years, then, every minute of every day, make sure that everything you do moves you in that direction. Not only will you feel a tremendous sense of progress, but you'll be happy, and you'll have more energy.

Goals are not merely matters of professional accomplishment. My wife, Barbara, and I decided that our goal was to raise happy, healthy, self-confident children, with high levels of self-confidence and self-esteem, who felt terrific about themselves. We decided that everything we did with our children would harmonize with that long-term goal: we would never do anything that would conflict with it.

We have stuck to that principle ever since our children were born. We've taken very good care of them physically, mentally, emotionally. We've always been present at their most important events, we've always told them how much we love them and believe in them, and we've always expressed our confidence in them. If they made mistakes, it was always just forgotten and let go.

One time my son Michael drove my car into a ditch. It had to be pulled out by a massive tow truck. I was out of the country. When I learned about it, I said, "It's OK. Life goes on."

Later he told me, "You have no idea how traumatic that was for me. After you had given me your car to drive, the first thing I did was drive it into a ditch, and you never said a word about it. I thought you were going to be furious." He'd seen all of his friends' parents and how they behaved.

But when I spoke to him on the phone, I said, "No, life goes on." When I got back, I got another car, and I let him use it. "Here's the car. Don't worry about it. Life goes on."

Years later, my son still remembers that. He said, "That was a real test: when you give your son your car, your son drives it into a ditch, and you never say a word."

That was how I had decided to be with my children: I would give them unconditional love, I would never criticize them, and when they made mistakes, I would let them go. I've always been happy about that.

When people asked me, "What do you do?" I used to say, "My main job is to raise my four children to be happy, healthy children and to be a good husband. Then I do some work on the side."

I see parenting as the central role of my life, because at the end of the day, that's all that's left. If you raise your children so they're happy, healthy, and positive and laugh a lot, and their children laugh a lot, you know you've done a good job. If you've given them everything else in the world, but they have negative personalities, they're unsure, or they lack self-confidence, to that degree you've failed as a parent.

Children are "love-tropic." Just as a sunflower bends toward the sun, children bend toward the major source of love and approval in their lives. Love and approval are, to a child, as important as oxygen or blood to the brain. Therefore, if you want to be the most important influence in your child's life, be the most important source of love and approval, so that your children always see you as the most positive part of their lives.

Your children will be influenced by their friends, schools, and relationships, but make sure that you are

---

If you want to be the most important influence in your child's life, be the most important source of love and approval.

---

the one who remains as their primary source of love and approval. I told my kids, "Your other friends will come and go. Some will be friends longer and some shorter, but your mother and I are never going anywhere. We will always be here. We will always be your best friends. We will always be near to take care of you. You can always count on us."

This is what we told our children when they were younger, and at a certain point they realized that friends do come and go. My daughter was sharing an apartment with another woman at the University of Miami. The roommate didn't have as much money as we do, so we paid for her to come on vacation with us to Hawaii and Cabo San Lucas. We took as good care of her as we did of our own children.

One day the roommate announced to my daughter that she was leaving. She was moving to another state, and she wouldn't be back. The roommate had a boyfriend. The boyfriend had decided to leave, so she decided to leave with him. She just up and left, never came back, and never communicated again.

My daughter had thought that this woman was her best friend. I said, "I told you before: your friends will come and go, and some of them will be better friends; some will be worse friends."

At this point, my daughter has seen lots of best friends forever—BFFs—come and go and then disappear.

They never come back, never communicate. But her parents are always at the end of the phone, an email, or a text message: her parents are always there.

I think all of our children realize that their parents are their best friends, because they can always count on us. This enables them to go through all kinds of difficulties. As long as they know that their parents are the single, most reliable source of love, approval, and influence in their lives, they're solid as rocks.

Sometimes kids are not sure of this parental love and approval. Last week the parents were fine, and this week they're really angry. How will they be next week? This unpredictability causes a child to grow up unstable, neurotic, insecure, angry, unsure, and distrusting of other people. The child finds it difficult to enter into long-term relationships with both sexes.

Children need to know that their parents will always be there for them; nothing will ever change that.

You have to set goals with regard to your children. You decide that in order to raise happy, healthy, self-confident children, you will do only those things that raise happy, healthy children, and you will not do things that do not. Your children's mental, emotional, and physical well-being takes precedence over everything else, because everything else will come and go. My oldest child is thirty-seven. That was my philosophy when she was born, and it's never deviated. It's the best thing of all if you have that as a central core of your life: that your family and your children are the most important.

The people you love and the people who love you are the most important things in life. If that is your anchor, if you're very clear about that, if you never do anything to violate that, everything else will take care of itself.

People ask about goals in relation to health and self-care. Everybody knows that the keys here are to eat good food, drink lots of water, and get regular exercise and lots of rest.

Research has found that wealthy people sleep eight and a half hours a night, while poor people sleep six or seven. Why? It's like the little battery on your phone: it has to be fully charged when you start your day. If you only get it three-quarters charged, it wears down. You no longer think as clearly, you're no longer as sharp, and you're no longer as patient. Rich people take more vacations than poor people, and they take more time off. That doesn't mean you don't have to work hard to be successful, but you have to balance work and leisure.

Successful people eat more nutritious foods, drink more liquids, and exercise every day. You need 200 minutes of exercise a week, which is about thirty minutes of walking per day. You take a thirty-minute walk each day, eat good foods, avoid sugars and desserts, take good care of your teeth, and get regular medical checkups.

Of course, this is all common knowledge. The challenge is self-discipline. Self-discipline is a matter of taking things one day at a time. Don't try to change the world; don't try to commit to change in your whole life; use the words "Just for today": Just for today, I will drink much more water. Just for today, I will only have two cups of coffee. Just for today, I will park my car two blocks away from my office, walk the distance, and walk up the stairs.

It's practice. Do a little bit each day until it becomes automatic. As Goethe said, "Everything is hard before it's easy." Say, "This will be hard to start with, and then it will be easy. I'll just start now, one step at a time."

If I offered you $1 million to walk a thousand miles—if you had to walk, not hitchhike or buy a plane ticket—how would you do it? You would go out of your door, and you would put one foot in front of the other. That's it. Some people will get there faster, and some people will get there more slowly, but everybody will get there. Just take it one step at a time.

The greatest challenge in life is always taking the first step. Once you do, the second step is easy. And you can always see the first step; it's always clear. Take the first step, then take the second step. Keep doing that, and eventually you can walk around the world.

You cannot influence others more than you can influence yourself. You have to have very strong willpower and self-discipline in order to exert influence on others. You must be very clear about who you are and what your strengths and weaknesses are, and about what you want, about your goals and how to reach them. You have to write them down; they cannot be like cigarette smoke in the air. You have to develop a plan to achieve your goals, one at a time—a financial goal, a health goal, a family goal. You have to work on these goals every day.

The keys to success are very simple: Decide exactly what you want, and write it down. Make a plan in detail. Take action on your plan, and work on it every day until you succeed. Resolve in advance that you'll never give up.

If you do these things, you will become an example to yourself. You will begin making progress towards your goals and will have more optimism and self-confidence. As a result, you will have more influence on other people, because they'll want to be more like you. They'll be more open to your guidance, because they see you making progress. Nothing makes you more influential than looking successful. People want to be like that, so they'll want to be like you.

Following this simple course of action will raise your self-esteem and self-confidence. You'll feel great about yourself, you'll accomplish extraordinary things, and you will be a role model and a person of influence in the lives of everyone around you.

**Keys to developing self-discipline
in order to influence others:**

- Be clear about who you are, including strengths and weaknesses.
- Write down your goals.
- Develop a plan to reach them, one step at a time.
- Work your plan every day until you succeed; never give up.

2

The Second Quality: Integrity

The second characteristic of influential people is *integrity*. Integrity is probably the most important quality for success in business and in life. Eighty-five percent of success in life is based on our relationships, and our relationships are based on trust. If the trust is not there, the relationship is not there, so integrity is everything. Your mother told you to always tell the truth. I say, first of all, live in truth with yourself, tell the truth to yourself, and live in truth with other people. Be a person of integrity.

If you want to have influence, be the kind of person that people know they can trust 100 percent. They know that you will never tell anybody else what they say to you

---

"If you want to have influence, be the kind of person that people know that they can trust 100%." —Brian Tracy

---

(even if they don't say, "This is really confidential"). It will never come back to them.

When you have influence, people trust you. I believe it was management guru Peter Drucker who said that when you come down to the main point, it's credibility; it's trust. The more people trust and like you, the more doors they will open for you. The first question people ask is, "Can you trust this person?"

You achieve everything that you achieve with the help of someone else. At every turning point in your life, you'll have somebody standing there. A person will open a door for you, or you'll call somebody, and they will call somebody who will open a door.

Your reputation is the most important thing in your career. Theodore Levitt of the Harvard Business School wrote a classic book called *The Marketing Imagination*. He said that integrity, or the reputation of a company, is its most valuable financial asset. The products and services can come and go, the executives can come and go, the financial statements can be good or bad over time, but the reputation—which are the words that people use to describe this company—remains a constant. It's like the roof and walls of your home: you can change the furniture, the lighting, and the colors, but the basic skeleton stays the same. So it is with your reputation.

Companies have to be very careful with anything that can affect their reputation, which is determined by the quality of their products or services. Your reputation consists of what people say about your company and your products. For a product to be successful, it has to be good: it has to achieve goals for people, it has to get results, and people have to be happy with those results. Eighty-five percent of the reason customers buy a product is word of mouth: Someone in the marketplace has bought the product, has used it, and has "good-mouthed" it: "This is a great product. This is phenomenal."

What do people say behind your back? Everybody has a position in the minds and hearts of others. Everybody in your company has an idea about who you are. Whenever we think of somebody else, we instantly see a picture of that person. We think of their interactions with us, what they've done, what they haven't done. All these thoughts come together and crystallize into a single idea about that individual. This determines whether we buy from them, meet with them, take their phone calls, hire them, promote them, pay attention to them, and respect them.

Another rule is that everything counts. Everything you say or don't say, everything you do or don't do—that counts. What is your reputation as a person? What is your company's reputation? What is the reputation of its individual products? At McDonald's, a Big Mac has a reputation that's different from that of a Filet-O-Fish, a salad, or french fries. The reputation of each product will determine whether or not people buy it, whether they will buy it again, and whether they tell their friends about it.

I have twenty-seven people who work in my organization selling products online, and we have a successful business. It works, and it's growing every week. We have 2.6 million people on our database, so we're approached by people asking, "Please, let us send out a promotion to your database." We ask them a number of questions.

One thing we insist on—which clears the decks quite quickly—is that everything that we offer has an unconditional money-back guarantee. We sell programs for education, financial investments, languages, goal setting, and time management. If you take the program, you get a specific result. If you don't, there is no charge. We've done that now for almost thirty-five years.

When I first started in this line, the Internet didn't exist, so I had to guarantee satisfaction just to get work. I would say, "I will speak for your organization, and if you're not happy, there's no charge." That made it incumbent upon me to design an excellent program, deliver it with energy, and make the audience happy. When you have the sword of no payment hanging over your head, you do a great job.

To build trust with customers, every product your company offers should be unconditionally guaranteed.

Any product that you provide should be unconditionally guaranteed. If someone says this product can improve your life or work in some way, they should stand behind their claim. I've always felt that that's the best testimony to your confidence in your product.

Many companies say, "You have to make this product work. We provide you with everything you need, but then it's up to you." I took a different approach. I started giving one-month guarantees and later one-year guarantees. I said, "You can take these programs and try them out. If you're not happy over the course of a year, you can send them back and get 100 percent of your money back, no charge, no questions."

I learned this concept from one of the biggest and best multilevel marketing companies. They had an empty-bottle guarantee: you could use their product; you could empty the bottle. If you weren't happy, you could bring the empty bottle back and get a 100 percent return, no questions asked. I thought, "That's a great guarantee."

The greatest single obstacle to real, lasting success is the idea that it's possible to get something for nothing. Good parents raise their children with the understanding that

---

**How can I contribute more value to my business
or my customers today?**

---

there's no such thing as something for nothing: you get out of life exactly what you put in. Your rewards will always be equal to the efforts that you put in, so the more efforts you put in, the more results you achieve, and the greater your rewards will be. If you want to earn more money, you have to put in greater effort. You have to increase your ability to produce results that people will pay you for. Ask yourself, what is the one thing that I can do today that will help me the most to get results that people will pay me for?

Peter Drucker said, "The word that will change your life is the word *contribution*." Some people think about making money or being successful, but you have to think about contribution. How can I contribute more value to my business or my customers today? How can I put more in?

When I studied economics, psychology, and metaphysics, I learned that the law of sowing and reaping is absolute. We call it the *law of cause and effect*, and it goes back to Aristotle in the fourth century BC. This law says that the more that you put in, the more you'll get out. If you want to increase the amount that you get out, you have to increase the quality and quantity of what you put in.

If you say, "I want to double my income," you have to double the value of your contribution. How can you do that? You can physically work more, or you can increase the intellectual value of your contribution. You can do more things of higher value. You can develop new skills that enable you to make a more valuable contribution, which benefits and rewards people, improving their lives in some way. The most successful people are those who throw their whole hearts into serving others.

I have an idea for a book called *The -Er Factor*. It's based on the idea that we achieve success by making our customers happy. If you make your customers happy with your product, they will buy it and buy it again. However, we live in a competitive world, so your competitors also want to make your customers happy. In order to lure them away from you, your competitors have to make your customers happi*er*.

How do you make them happier? You have to serve them *faster*, like Amazon or Domino's Pizza. You have to serve them items of *higher* quality, like Tiffany's or Lululemon sports clothes. There always has to be an -*er*. Better, smarter, faster, easier, more convenient—"convenient-*er*"—it's always the comparative. You have to offer the customer something that is so important that they will choose to buy from you rather than anyone else. Your job is to always look for ways to add an -*er* to the equation. Sometimes it can be polit*er*, pleasant*er*, clean*er*.

People think that a company's bathrooms will be at the same level of cleanliness as the parking lot, so they look at the parking lot. If it's clean, they assume that the bathrooms will be clean, so they can stop with their family and eat there. This is why McDonald's parking lots are so clean: people will assume their restrooms are cleaner than the competitors'. So you have to keep asking: what can we do to get an -*er* factor?

Remember that everybody is greedy, selfish, ambitious, vain, ignorant, and impatient. Everyone is always asking, "What's in it for me? How can I benefit?" Every ad that you send out is an attempt to influence people to take an action that they would not have taken in the absence of your communication. When they see an ad, the first thing people want to know is "What's in it for me?"

Your slogan must show that if the customer buys your product or service, the improvements in their lives will be quick, immediate, desirable, valuable, and superior to the results offered by competitors.

In economics, *scarcity is everything*. People have limited money, time, resources, and energy. They want to get the very most for the very least, so they are constantly looking for products and services that will improve their lives at the lowest possible cost in the fastest possible way.

All marketing today is an attempt to hit that sweet spot and get people to say, "Aha! I want that offering, and I want it now." It's a matter of getting them to pay attention and then getting them to respond, purchase the product, use it, and be so happy with it that they buy it again.

In marketing today, you usually have to offer people something that is free, inexpensive, or guaranteed. I have a good friend who has a successful online business. He buys key words from Google, for example *self-confidence*, and he'll add an exclamation point or question mark. A person who lacks self-confidence will turn to that key word. They click on *self-confidence!* "How would you like to have more self-confidence, to be unafraid in every situation, to speak clearly and articulately, and to have people take notice, be influenced by your arguments, and buy your products and services?"

A person says, "Yes, yes, I want that."

"Click here." They'll offer a module on self-confidence, saying, "The person who takes the action achieves the goal, so action is central to developing and maintaining self-confidence. For more, click here," and the site will lead to a couple of paragraphs on action. Then it will march people through a funnel so they will conclude that if they want to develop self-confidence, they should read the book that is being marketed.

You have to start off saying, "Is this something that you would want? If it is, here's a little taste of what you would get." You have to lead them step by step so that the person starts to believe, "Yes, if I do these things, I will have greater self-confidence, and I will influence people; people will listen to me; people will do what I suggest." Eventually you sell them the product.

The whole purpose of marketing is to offer a product that people want and need instantly. They feel that if they had more self-confidence, they could ask for a raise, they could ask a girl out on a date, they could set bigger goals, they could close more sales, they could fire an unsatisfactory employee. All marketing is based on offering something that people want here and now.

Here's another point: You try to influence people who already want and need the product or service. You don't try to find people who may want or need the product or service sometime in the future; you want to find people who need the product or service at this moment.

Say you sell hand-held fire extinguishers, and you meet a man whose hair is on fire. He is a good prospect: he is a person who wants and needs a fire extinguisher, and he wants and needs it now. He's willing to pay almost any price for it. The benefits of getting the fire

---

Try to focus your time on influencing people who already want and need your product or service.

---

extinguisher are so enormous that he's willing to make a buying decision immediately.

That's what you're looking for in a customer: somebody who wants it and needs the product, who can use it and afford it the minute you present to them.

3

The Third Quality: Attitude

The third quality of influential people is that they have a great *attitude*. Researchers interviewed the founders of the 500 fastest-growing companies in America and found that one common quality they had was extreme optimism.

Insprational speaker Earl Nightingale said the most important word in the language is *attitude*, because it's the first thing that people feel and sense about you. Napoleon Hill started off his classic book *Think and*

"The most important word in the English language is *attitude*." —Earl Nightingale

Grow Rich by emphasizing the importance of a positive mental attitude.

First and foremost, a positive mental attitude is a positive response to stress. Your life is full of many ups and downs and difficulties, but you should be generally positive and cheerful in response to stress. Look for the good. Look for the valuable lesson in every situation. Rise above problems and difficulties.

You can also decide not to have negative emotions. People are trained to believe that both negative emotions and positive emotions are normal and natural parts of life: if you have some of one, you have some of the other. If you have the negative, you have the positive, and if you have the positive, you have the negative. It's normal, like breathing.

That's not true. Negative emotion is a decision. You can decide not to be negative. Say, "I don't have negative emotions."

People ask me, "What do you do when you're depressed? How do you respond when you're down?"

I said, "I'm never depressed. I'm never negative."

I notice other people who seem to be positive all the time, and I ask, "Have you ever had a problem with being negative?"

"No, I'm never negative."

"What about when things go against you?"

"I'm never negative."

You too can decide that you will always persevere in the face of difficulty, you will never be negative, you will always keep going, and you will always be a positive person. Just make the decision once, and it locks in. From then on, you don't have to question it. In any situation where there's a possibility of feeling negative, something in your subconscious mind immediately kicks in, and the feeling is gone.

Some people are concerned that their success may be impeded by a dysfunctional background, say, from sexual or physical abuse. Let me give you the bottom line: almost everybody has had a dysfunctional upbringing of some kind. Each child comes into the world as a clean slate. They have no negative emotions, no anger, frustration, or phobias. The only instinctive fears that a child has are the fear of falling and the fear of loud noises, which are normal and natural.

Early in life, children start to develop two negative habit patterns. A negative habit pattern is an automatic response to a stimulus in the environment. One pattern they develop is the *fear of failure*, which comes about when the parent says, "No, stop," and shouts, slaps, punishes, or hurts the child for doing something the parent dislikes. Children have only one need, and that is for love and security, so if their parents shout and scream at them, it terrifies them. They start to behave in whatever way will earn the unconditional support of their parents.

The greatest trauma for a child is love withheld.
The most important gift for a child is unconditional love.

The second negative pattern that children develop is the *fear of disapproval*. This comes about when the parent says, "Get away from that. Put that down. Leave that alone," and slaps or spanks the child. The child begins to develop the fear of rejection, the feeling "I can't, I can't, I can't."

Consequently, by the time the child is two or three, it has two negative patterns: *I can't*, and *I have to*. "I can't do what my parents don't want me to do, and I have to do what makes them happy." The parents are constantly criticizing and punishing the child for doing what they don't want them to do, or for not doing something they want them to do. The parents are constantly withdrawing their love.

A child needs love as roses need rain or the brain needs oxygen. The parent threatens to take away love by saying, "Get away from there. Stop that. Don't do that." Because the child needs love, it quickly develops a fear of rejection or disapproval. "If I don't do what my parents approve of, I will not be safe. I will lose their love, and I can die emotionally."

All negative behaviors in adulthood stem back to love withheld in childhood. The child is threatened with the withdrawal of the love it needs—it's like the withdrawal of the blood to the brain—so the most important gift for a child is unconditional love.

The greatest trauma for a child is love withheld. Worst of all is taking it away and offering it back, and then taking it away and offering it back again. The child becomes angry, fearful, unstable, because it never knows what to do or not to do to ensure the continuous flow of love. As a result, the child grows up with the fear of failure, the fear of making a mistake, and the fear of being punished. It grows up with the fear of rejection, risk, not being loved, not being safe. It develops a terrible fear of failure: "If I do something and I'm not successful, I will lose my parents' love, I won't be safe, I'll be in great danger. Or if I don't do what my parents approve of, I will be punished, and my love will be taken away, and I will be unsafe; I will be alone in a fearful world."

Those two fears grow up and mutate into fear of failure, fear of risk, fear of loss, fear of embarrassment, fear of disapproval, hypersensitivity, fear of the negative opinions of others. All of the major fears start from the fear of failure and fear of rejection.

A multimillionaire once told me that no matter how much he accomplishes, he has a private fear that it's all going to be taken away. This kind of fear is inculcated before the child is five years old. In most cases, the parents don't even know they're doing it. They just think

---

".....the great cancer that destroys the souls of human beings is destructive criticism." —Brian Tracy

---

they are controlling the child by threatening it with disapproval if it doesn't do what they want them to do. They don't realize that they're laying down this pattern.

I have four children. I know that the great cancer that destroys the souls of human beings is destructive criticism, so I have never criticized them. That doesn't mean that we don't fight, or argue, or disagree, but I never have said, "You are bad."

My children have gotten into trouble, they've been expelled, they've done all kinds of things that kids do. No matter what they did, I sat them down and asked, "What happened?" They were really nervous. I said, "Don't worry. It's OK. I did thing like that when I was young, so just tell me what happened, and let's get it out on the table."

They would tell me, and I'd say, "What are you going to do next time?"

"Next time I'm going to be more careful."

"That's great, because my parents would punish me terribly, and then they'd remind me about it for ten years. It was as if you were never forgiven."

With my kids, I said, "It happens." Years would go by, and I would joke with them and say, "Remember that time you did that?"

"Yes."

"That was a really crazy thing, wasn't it?"

"Yes." There's no negativity. There's nothing left over.

How do you deal with negative mental patterns if you're an adult? The core of your personality is your self-esteem: how much you like and love yourself. This in turn determines how much you love others. Start by saying, "I like myself."

This is probably one of the most eye-opening discoveries I have ever made. Each time you say, "I like myself; I love myself," your fears go down and your self-love goes up, like a teeter-totter, and you eventually reach the point where you love yourself unconditionally.

I've always told my children, "I love you unconditionally. There's nothing that you can ever do that could cause me to love you less than 100 percent." You have to repeat it for a while. This assurance is abstract to them until they face a real problem and their parents still stand behind them 100 percent.

Here is perhaps the most important insight in personal development: unwillingness or inability to forgive is the greatest single block to happiness. The most important thing you can do in life is to forgive everybody who's ever hurt you in any way. Let it go completely and realize that it has nothing to do with them; it has to do with you. Say, "I forgive my parents for every mistake they ever made in bringing me up. I forgive everyone in my life, my previous relationships, my siblings, my friends. I forgive my boss, and I forgive myself 100 percent."

The greatest message that Jesus taught in the New Testament was forgiveness. The one thing that you can do to stay completely clean of all negativity is to go through each person in your life and forgive them 100 percent for anything they ever did to hurt you.

Once a man called me from the Netherlands. He said he had been raised in a dysfunctional family. He was furious with them. He got married, had a bad marriage, was cheated by a partner, and lost all his money.

The man was sick; his heart was in trouble. He had the beginnings of cancer; he had every kind of illness. He went to the doctor, who told him, "You're going to die. Your system is shot. You've got about six months to live, and there's nothing that modern medicine can do for you, so you should make peace with the people in your life. You're still angry at many people. Just let them go."

The man made a list of thirty-nine people he was furious with. He went through the list and said, "All right, I'm going to forgive them." One by one he went through the list. He thought about how angry he had been and said, "I forgive this person completely." (He'd heard this advice in my program *The Psychology of Achievement*.) "I forgive

this person completely for everything, and I let them go."
He went through the list, name by name. Some names
were hard, but he persisted. Then he started back again
and realized that he would have to call or visit some of
these people.

The man put all his affairs in order, wrote his will,
and sold his clothes. Then he phoned and visited the people on his list, asked for their forgiveness, and forgave
them. He traveled to the United States and England. For
the next six months, he went around, forgiving people
and asking for their forgiveness. As he did this, his health
improved.

By the end of the six months, this man's mind, soul,
and heart were completely clear. He had forgiven every
single person that had ever hurt him. He had no negative feelings at all. He felt fabulous about himself, and he
had no pains. He went back to the doctor, who couldn't
believe it: "You are completely symptom-free."

Meanwhile the man had been working, and he was
starting to make more money than he had ever made.
He felt wonderful about himself, and he did not have a
single negative thought or feeling. He was a transformed
person. He resumed his life, and he felt fabulous.

What an incredible story! Decide that you're going to
freely forgive everybody who has ever hurt you for any
reason for the rest of your life.

Ideas to develop a great attitude

- Look for the valuable lesson in every situation.
- Reject negativity.
- Persevere in the face of difficulty.
- Raise children in a secure environment of unconditional love.
- Don't practice destructive criticism with yourself or others.
- Practice the self-talk "I like myself" and "I love myself."
- Be quick to forgive yourself and others.

4

The Fourth Quality: Sincerity

The fourth quality of influential people is that they are *sincere*. They always tell the truth, but they are also polite. I had a good friend who was honest but completely tactless: if he thought that something was wrong about somebody, he would criticize them. He said, "I'm just being sincere."

"No," I said, "you're not just being sincere. You're being rude, and you're hurting people's feelings."

"Well, I'm not going to lie."

"You don't have to lie, but you can keep your mouth shut."

For many years, Benjamin Franklin was outspoken and aggressive. He would argue with people, and he thought that the most important thing in a conversation was to win. Finally someone took him aside and said, "It's better to be liked than to be right. What does it matter if the other person's wrong, especially about a petty issue? Just let it go."

Instead of disagreeing with people, Franklin started to ask them, "That's an interesting point of view. Why do you feel that way? Please tell me your thinking on this subject, so that I can understand better."

As a result of this approach, people quickly changed from adversaries to friends. Moreover, Franklin often found that his own ideas were completely wrong, and others had much better ones. He learned to be so open and flexible that he became one of the most popular and influential men in the American colonies. His judicious, conscientious, and friendly nature was a critical factor in the formation of the American Union.

I used to be like Franklin: I was determined to win in any conversation. But at one point, I decided that in the future, I would never make a statement even when I was clearly right. Instead I would ask people to explain their thinking, and I would listen carefully to the answers.

Furthermore, never challenge the other person. I used to make this mistake. I'd say, "You may have thought about it, but you're wrong." I found that the worst thing

---

**Instead of disagreeing with others, ask them the
Benjamin Franklin question: "That's an interesting
point of view. Why do you feel that way?"**

---

you can tell another person is that they're wrong, because
it turns them off completely. If you don't challenge them
directly, they have the opportunity to back down from
their position.

A wonderful line says, "A man convinced against his
will is of the same opinion still." Even if you do win the
argument, you won't change the other person's mind; they
just won't like you. And one person at a critical moment
can have a negative influence on your future. They can
step in and say, "This is my chance to get even with this
guy." If you're applying for a loan, someone can say, "I
would never say that he was dishonest, because I don't
really have hard proof of it, but I would never say he's
honest either." Little things like that can undermine you.

One of the greatest problems in human life is trying to change people and get them to be other than they
are. Stop trying to change people. They aren't going to
change. You're not going to change, you haven't changed
in twenty-five years, so others aren't going to change
either. Just let it go.

You cannot make another person do something. You
cannot make anyone more ambitious, hard-working, or

**The more convinced that people are that they will
be better off, the more open they are to influence.**

---

punctual. There's nothing that you can do to change the
behavior of another person, so just let it go.

A person will only move, change, or take an action of
any kind if they feel that they are going to be better off
afterwards. The more convinced they are that they will
be better off, the more open they are to influence.

Imagine a business plaza with people walking to and
from their jobs and offices and meetings. You walk out
into the middle of the business plaza, and you have 100
$1 bills concealed in your hand. At a certain moment,
you suddenly throw the bills up into the air, and they flut-
ter down.

People look and see this free money floating in the
air. Within seconds, they go from normal to berserk—
shouting, grabbing, screaming, pushing. They are going
after this money because there's only a certain amount of
it. Other people are pursuing it. It will soon be gone. If
they don't move quickly, they won't get their share.

On some occasions, an armored car was driving
down the street, and a door came open on the back end.
Money poured out onto the street. Traffic stopped, and
people started coming from all directions, shouting,
fighting, and piling over one another.

All this money floating in the air was a form of influence. It instantaneously caused behavior that would never have taken place otherwise.

Another example from recent years is the release of a new Apple iPhone. The company announces that the phone will be available at eight o'clock on Saturday morning. The night before, people are sleeping on the street in front of the store to get the new phones first. There are even placeholders: people who for $5 will hold your place while you go to the bathroom or get some food. All of this occurs because people are so eager to get the product.

This is influence. People are so excited about an anticipated improvement that they will engage in behaviors that, from an outside point of view, seem to be almost insane.

Everyone has a desire to achieve the most, the fastest, and easiest way possible, with the least concern for secondary consequences. Furthermore, as the great twentieth-century psychologist Abraham Maslow said, every person has an inherent desire to fulfill their potential. A great metaphysical teacher once wrote that all frustration, anger, depression, and social problems come from a feeling that people have far more potential than they're currently using and don't know how to have access to it. It's as if they have a gold mine or an oil well on their property but have no idea of how to get to it.

When I was twenty-four or twenty-five, I started learning the psychology of selling. What thinking process

---

**The profession of Sales is influence
taken to its highest level.**

---

do people go through to be successful salespeople? What thinking process do you have to take people through for them to buy from you?

The same process turns out to apply worldwide: China, Russia, Africa, Asia, Europe, the United States. Sales is influence taken to its highest level. I'll give you the critical skills.

First, before you start talking to a person, you have to find out whether or not this person wants, needs, can use, and afford your product or service. You don't try to sell people on your product if they're obviously not interested or have no need for it. From casual conversation, you find out their goals, long-term objectives, problems, and current situation. At the same time, you're also building rapport and trust.

The first thing that a prospective customer looks for—indeed the first thing that anybody looks for when they meet another person—is warmth and trust. These are the most important qualities. Until these are established, the person has no interest in proceeding with you.

Former coach Lou Holtz used to say that before a person has any interest in talking to you, he wants to know the answer to the question, *do you care about me?* If you don't care about me, why should I care about you?

Be genuinely interested when you meet and shake hands with a person: "How are you? My name is Brian Tracy. What's your name?" It's a very simple opening for any kind of social interaction, because people like the sound of their own names. When they give you their name, you repeat it back.

If you are meeting with a prospect in sales, you can say, "Thank you very much for your time. I know how busy you are. Is this still a good time for you?" People appreciate the fact that you respect their time.

Interviewing customers, we've found that after they've made an appointment with a salesperson they don't know, they wish they hadn't, because they're so busy. When a prospect encounters a salesperson, it's really an interruption. This is the case even when they've agreed to see the person, because they have so many other things to do. So say, "Thank you for your time. I know how busy you are. Is this still a good time?" You're acknowledging that they are busy and that you are interrupting them, so they are disposed to like you from the get-go.

"Before a person has any interest in talking to you,
he or she wants to know the answer to the question,
do you care about me?" —Lou Holtz

You ask, "How are you?"

"Fine."

"How is your business today?" You start with general, impersonal questions. You don't ask people about their families when you've just met them for the first time.

As the person answers, you nod and listen. Ask a question, and listen closely to the answer: lean forward intently, as though the answer is important to you. Most people are poor listeners: they ask a question just to fill the space, and they're waiting for you to finish answering so they can go on speaking. Good listeners ask a question and then listen. They lean in closely, as though the answer is very important to them and they really want to know it.

Step number one in effective selling is to listen intently, nod, smile, pay attention, and listen without interrupting. This usually surprises people. Most listening is not really listening; it's just waiting. You ask a person a question, but you're really waiting for them to stop talking so you can jump in with your two cents' worth.

The second key is to pause before replying. When the person finishes speaking, you don't just jump in and start speaking at 100 miles an hour. You pause, listen carefully, say "Uh-huh," and think about what the person just said, as if what they said was important. Because if what they said was important, then by extension they must be important. Again, the great rule for human relations is to make people feel important.

The third point is to ask questions for clarification. The very best question of all is, "What do you mean?" or "What do you mean exactly?" Give the person a chance to answer. When they expand on their answer, you listen closely, nod, smile, and again make no attempt to interrupt. Then you can ask follow-up questions.

The fourth key is to feed back what the person is saying in your own words: "Oh, so what you're doing right now is this, and this is what's happening and how it's working out. Is that correct?"

"Yes, that's my situation."

"May I ask you a question?" Remember, the person who asks questions has control, so the most powerful way to build a relationship is to ask questions, lean forward, listen intently to the answers, pause before replying, and then ask further questions.

If the prospect asks you a question, pause and say, "That's a very good question. May I ask you something first?"

You always answer a question with a question. The person who asks questions has control. Listening builds trust, so if you keep asking questions, leaning forward, and listening intently to the answers, the person starts to like and trust you more and more. The more you ask questions and listen, the more the customer trusts you and the more open they are.

When you first meet the customer, they have very high levels of skepticism and fear, because they have made buying mistakes in the past. They've bought the wrong thing and they've paid too much, so they're cautious. People are suspicious today: their level of fear is high, and your level of credibility is very low at first. The more you ask questions and listen intently to the answers, the more the prospect will like you and trust you. The more their fear goes down, the more their confidence in you goes up.

You can take a person who is skeptical, negative, reserved, and restrained and turn them into a genuinely interested prospect just by asking good questions, pausing, listening closely to the answers, asking more questions for clarification, and keeping the cycle going. The starting point is listening.

As the research has shown, at a certain point the customer will feel so comfortable with you that they'll ask you questions about yourself. If you start talking about your product before they invite you to, you'll kill the sale. Many salespeople make this mistake: They meet the prospect and say, "Hello. How are you?"

"Fine."

"How's life?"

"Good."

"How's your business?"

"Wonderful."

"Thank you very much for your time, because I think I have something for you that you'll really like." They immediately launch into talking about their product or service.

But this is too soon. At this point, you just keep asking questions until the customer is so completely relaxed with you that they will say, "Tell me what you've got; tell me why you're here," "What can I do for you?" or "What have you got?"

You say, "Thank you very much. I think we can be of great help to you. Let me ask you a couple of questions. What are you doing now in this area, and how is that working for you?"

Step one is focused on questions that are general and nonspecific: How's business going? How's the economy affecting you? What did you think about the election? How is it going to affect your business? What kind of competition are you experiencing? Ask general questions, as you would at a reception or a social event.

At a certain stage, you move away from the personal. Researchers have found, in reviewing tens of thousands of videotaped sales conversations, that the customer will reach the point where they'll invite you to shift into talking about the reason for your visit. If you start talking about your product too soon, before the customer has indicated that they're comfortable and want to hear about it, you can kill the sale. Up to that point, just listen, nod, smile, and ask more questions. At a certain point they'll say, "Why don't you tell me a little bit about what you have?"

It's like a semaphore on an aircraft carrier. The prospect will wave the flags and say, "Now it's time to start talking about your product." If you start too early, the prospect will think, "We were just getting to know each other, and then he immediately started talking about his product. It was too soon."

It's like meeting an attractive girl, sharing a few courtesies, and then pouncing on her and trying to kiss her. There may be a time for that, but this is too soon. In terms of sales, you have not established enough of a relationship to start talking about exchanging money for promises.

When the customer invites you to talk about your product, you say, "Before I can tell you anything about what I've got, may I ask you a couple of questions about what you're doing now?" Good salespeople have predetermined questions that go from the general to the specific. Poor salespeople say whatever falls out of their mouths, but professional salespeople ask, "Can you tell me a little bit about what you're doing in this area now? How are you handling this problem, need, job, or service? How is that working for you? Are you happy with the results that you're getting now?"

**Influential salespeople ask their prospects:
"How is your current product or service working for you?
If you could change anything about it, what would
you want to change?"**

After all, people only move in order to increase their level of satisfaction, so in psychological terms, a person must have a level of felt dissatisfaction. An individual is not a genuine prospect unless they are unhappy with their current situation. At that point, they're open to a product or service that will help them.

Instead of assuming that the prospect needs your product or service, ask them, "How is your current product or service working for you? If you could change anything about it, what would you want to change; what would you want to have more of, or less of?"

You're exploring to see if there's a gap. We call this a *gap analysis*: a gap between where the customer is now and where the customer could be with your product or service. If the customer says, "I'm perfectly happy with my existing supplier and don't need anything else; thank you very much for coming in," this is obviously not a prospect for you.

What do you do if your prospect says they're perfectly happy with their existing supplier, who is taking care of everything they need? Move on, because that is the ideal: to get a customer and take such good care of them that they're loyal and not interested in buying from anyone else. If you ever meet someone who's like that, accept it as a reality and move on. Say, "It sounds like you're so happy with what you're doing that there's really no way that I can improve your situation, so thank you very much for your time. If ever you do need something different, if ever I can be of any help to you, here's my business card. We have a lot of different approaches that cause our product to be seen as superior, but you can decide for yourself."

Sometimes the customer will reply, "Tell me a little bit more about what you have and about how your product is different," because it may turn out that they are not entirely happy with the current service, or they're open to changing. Eight out of ten users of products and services feel they can be better off with another one. They just don't know what it is or how they could be better off.

Which brings us to an interesting point. Destructive criticism is the greatest destroyer of human souls, so you never criticize at any stage of a sales conversation. You never criticize your company, of course, you never criticize anything on the market, and you never criticize your competitor.

I didn't know this when I was starting off. A prospect would say, "I'm using this competitor." I would say, "Gee, those people, they're no good there, they're bad here, and they charge too much." I would pull up as many criticisms as I could.

Then I learned—and this is a shocker—that when you criticize the current supplier of your customer, you're actually criticizing the customer, who made the decision to buy from them. You're saying that they were dumb because they bought from this other supplier, whereas if you buy from me, you'll be smart again.

Never say that. Do the opposite. If they say they're using a competitor, always be complimentary. Say, "That's a good company. They've been in business for a long time. They do wonderful work. I've heard a lot of good things about them." Then say, "We approach your situation from a slightly different direction, and our customers appreciate our approach, because we enable them to do certain things that are not possible with our competitors. But you're with a good company."

Always point out that although you take a different (and superior) approach, the prospect's current choice is good. It's a good company. They've been in business a long time. The prospect will often say, "They're not that great, because I've had several problems with service." They will then tell you their areas of dissatisfaction with your competitor and ask, "What can you do about that?"

You say, "Well, it's interesting, because I've heard that problem before. The way we handle it is . . ." and you talk about how you help the customer to be much better off by solving the problem. In any event, never say anything negative about your competitor.

One of the things I teach is called the Golden Triangle of Selling. It's based on interviews with tens of thousands of customers, who are asked, "What do you think of these salespeople you have bought from in the past?" And we know that these are the top salespeople in that company.

These three words describe influential salespeople, and comprise The Golden Triangle of Selling:

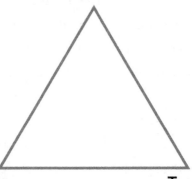

Friend
The salesperson cares more about me
than making the sale.

Advisor
I don't think the salesperson is
trying to sell me, so much as to
help me improve my situation.

Teacher
I see him or her more as a
teacher than a salesperson.

The customers come up with three words. The first word is "I see him or her as a *friend* rather than as a salesperson. I think that this person cares more about me than making a sale, so I see him or her as a friend in that industry."

The second word is "I see him or her as an *advisor* or a helper. I don't think that he is trying to sell me so much as help me to improve my situation. I see him as a consultant, a problem solver"—because, remember, the purchase of every product is a solution to a problem of some kind.

How does the customer get the impression that you're more concerned about their problems than the sale? It's because you ask them about their problems with the product all the time: How are you doing in this area? How is that working for you? Are you having any problems or difficulties? What are the biggest problems you're having?

Sometimes I say, "Imagine you can wave a magic wand over this situation so it would be perfect in every way. How would it be different from today? What would you have more of, or less of? If your situation regarding this product were perfect, how would it be different?"

Very often they'll say, "If my situation was perfect, I would want to do more of this or less of that." This will give you openings. Again, it will show you the gap between where the customer wants to be and where they feel they are today. This is a very good way of positioning yourself as a problem solver: looking for ways to help them. A good salesperson always sees themselves as a helper rather than as a salesperson.

The third word customers use is *teacher*. "I see him or her more as a *teacher* than as a salesperson."

We call these processes *relationship selling*, where you position yourself as a friend; *consultative selling*, where you position yourself as an advisor; and *educational selling*, where you position yourself as a teacher.

IBM became the biggest computer supplier in the world. They had 82 percent of the world computer market until more and more companies got into the business. Before that point, there were a lot of companies that had similar products, even superior products, but still IBM managed to hold on to 82 percent of the market. The federal government even tried to bring antitrust charges against them.

Analysts studied the way that IBM salespeople dealt with their customers. They were always coming in with different ideas about how you could use the computer to get more advantages, more services—how the computer could enable you to accomplish certain tasks, how you could do more document processing, how you could do multiple documents and two-sided documents, how you could prepare documents and combine them with other documents.

You didn't just buy the machine and have it there. The IBM people would call on a regular basis and say, "Did you know that IBM has now added this feature, so you can do this additional thing that you weren't able to do before?" IBM kept the customer feeling that the value of the computer they owned was going up and up, and that IBM was constantly increasing its value by coming back and showing them how to get even more out of it. Soon all the successful companies would do the same thing. They're constantly showing the customer how they can get more value.

In a sales presentation, the first thing is to show a problem or need that the prospect has and that this product or service will satisfy this need or take this problem away. The presentation might also describe some of the things the prospect can do with this product or service that they may not have been able to do in the past: "This will dramatically increase the speed at which you achieve your goals, process your documents, service your customers, manufacture your products, and increase the speed of your repairs. We're constantly upgrading the product, so you will constantly be getting new, more, better, faster, easier features that you can use to get greater value from the product." People constantly feel that the product that they've bought is becoming more and more valuable. That's how you make a presentation.

Research has also found that the primary emotion holding a customer back from buying is the fear of risk. Risk is everything, because everybody wants the benefits of a product, but what about the risk? What if the prod-

---

Key Benefit = What are all of the reasons that the customer *will* buy?

Key Fear = What are all of the reasons that the customer *won't* buy?

---

uct doesn't work out? What if I buy it, and it turns out not to do what it's supposed to do? What if I find it costs less somewhere else?

You ask, what are all the reasons a person *will* buy, and what are all the reasons they *won't* buy? We call these two things the *key benefit*, the thing that will make a person buy—there's usually one—and the *key fear*, the key risk in the customer's mind that holds them back from buying.

You emphasize the key benefit, and you also deal with the fear: "We have an unconditional money-back guarantee complete with service for the first twelve months. After that, we have a service contract at a minor cost that will ensure that we keep your product up and working. There will be somebody here to help you resolve a problem of any kind within two hours, should you have one."

One of your primary jobs is to emphasize the benefits and take away the idea of risk: when you buy this product from us, you never have to worry about it again. That's why the most successful companies today—the

Amazons, the Apples—give unconditional guarantees. Guarantees are important, because if there's no risk to buying the product and it includes all the benefits that are being promised, I should order it now. That's the end of a good sales presentation: the customer says, "I want it now. I'm ready. How soon can I get it?"

The final part of a sales presentation is, of course, the close—the ultimate form of influence in the sales process. The ideal is to establish so much value that customer feels their only option is to proceed. You just say, "Do you have any questions or concerns that I haven't covered? No? Well, then let's get going. How soon would you need this? Would you want it delivered to your home or your office?"

The close is very gentle, very easy, no stress, no pressure at all. You have the customer agree that they want to use and enjoy everything that you've described, so let's get started.

Today everything is Internet, everything is email, everybody's buying everything online. How, then, can you reach customers?

Recent statistics indicate that only 11 percent of sales are taking place online. This is shocking, because people think that everybody's buying everything online.

Here's what research has found. There are two major types of product sales, like two weights on a dumbbell—

transactions and *tailored items*. At one end of the barbell is what are called *transactions*. I tell you about a book, a camera, or a pair of shoes, so you go online and buy it. A transaction does not require deep meditation, a discussion with your family, or going to the mountaintop and lighting a candle.

An enormous number of products are sold transactionally: we've decided to buy them, so we go online. We find out where they are and how much they cost in comparison to competing products. Then we choose a product and buy it. We click at the bottom of the web page, the product is mailed to us, and we get on with our day. We're doing more and more buying this way, instead of going to stores. Thirty percent of shopping centers in the U.S. are closing down or being repurposed into bowling alleys, movie theaters, churches, and health clubs, because people don't go to shopping centers anymore. They can buy those products online. That's transactional.

At the other end of the barbell are *tailored items*, which are specific to an individual. For example, you may decide that you need a laptop computer, but you may not be sure which one you need, so you'll go to the Apple store (which is why Apple stores now are the highest-grossing retail stores per square foot in the world).

But say you need a shirt, a tie, a suit, or a set of earphones, and you're not sure what sort you want. In these cases, you want to go to a specialty store and physically

Transactions

Transactions are purchases made over and over with little reflection required by the consumer. Typically not customized to the consumer, but mass-marketed. Easily purchased online.

Tailored Items

Tailored items are purchases that are customized to the individual or require further consultation and consideration before purchasing. More likely to require a real-life salesperson.

look at the item. You're not going to buy office furniture or equipment online; nor are you going to buy special printing for advertising promotions. You're going to find a supplier online, you're going to call them, and you're going to ask them to send someone over to see you.

In short, the market for real-life salespeople is huge and getting larger, because there are so many products available. With transactional products, about which a person knows everything they need to know, they go online and they can make a decision. With nontransactional products, products that are customized and tailored, the customers want to see and talk to a salesperson.

Imagine trying to do interior decorating for your home online. You may do some research to find who the best people are, so they have to have an online presence, but you have to speak to somebody personally to make sure that you like them, trust them, and believe that they're credible, competent, and capable.

Purchasers look for two things. The first is trust and warmth. The second thing is strength and competence. Researchers have determined that people make decisions about trust and warmth within five to seven seconds. But they make their decisions with regard to strength, ability, and competence over a longer period of time—sometimes after two or three meetings. To get in the door, you have to be warm, likable, and trustworthy, but to make the sale, you have to demonstrate that you can give sound advice and give the customer good ideas about their choices.

5

The Fifth Quality:
Being Well-Informed

The fifth quality of influential people is that they are *well-informed*, both overall and about their specific professions. Today information is doubling at a rate of about two or three times a year. It has been estimated that 90 percent of all the people who have ever done research and writing are alive and working today. When I began writing books in 1989, about 240,000 books a year were being published. Today the figure is more than 5 million books a year, and many of them are by the smartest and best-informed people in their

---

Brian Tracy's formula for staying well informed: *Get up an hour early every morning and read to upgrade your skills.*

---

fields. Some of these books are beautiful pieces of writing, with insights that can save a person ten years of hard work.

If you're not continually reading and keeping informed, you're not staying even, you're falling behind. It's like being on a treadmill: if it keeps going and you don't, you fall further and further behind. If the treadmill speeds up (which it is), you have to speed up just to stay even.

The formula for keeping well-informed is simple: get up an hour early every morning and read to upgrade your skills. I read about thirty magazines a month and three or four newspapers a day. I listen to educational audio programs in my car and watch educational DVDs and educational television as well. I consume about three hours' worth of information per day. I get up in the morning and do two or three hours of reading; I also read on weekends. On an eight-hour flight, I will read and make notes for five hours.

By continuing to read, I'm developing new intellectual content. I have now written eighty books, without notes. I sit down, clear my desk, lay all of my material out, and then write. I write the books from cover to cover with no notes, because I have all of the information in my brain.

A recent study found that wealthy people read one hour per day or more and watch only one hour of television. Charlie Munger, a friend of Warren Buffett's, says, "If you are not continuing to read, you have no chance in the twenty-first century." For success today, you need what he calls "deep learning," which means taking the time to go deeply into a subject. You cannot accomplish this by flitting across little tidbits of knowledge on the Internet. You have to take the time to read books; you have to dig deep into a subject to be able to keep current with it.

"If you are not continuing to read, you have no chance (of success) in the 21st Century." —Charlie Munger

---

If you're not continually reading, if you're not continually upgrading your skills and knowledge, you have no future; you're living on borrowed time. Warren Buffett is said to spend 80 percent of his time reading every day. He goes to work, shuts off all interruptions, puts his head down, and spends about most of his time reading. In between times he'll check telephone calls, messages, a little bit of email. He doesn't go on social media. He reads all the time. That's why he can make brilliant multibillion-dollar decisions.

Another one of the richest men in the world is Carlos Slim, the Warren Buffett of Mexico. He started with very little, built up a successful concrete distribution business, and became a billionaire. He too studies 60 to 70 percent of every day.

Being well-informed makes you much more confident. A well-informed person who goes into a business meeting is a very different person from one who is not. *Power is on the side of the person with the best information.* If you go into a meeting, and the other person has better information than you, they've got the power. Never allow that to happen. Do your homework.

Being well-informed is connected to the most important relationship of all: the one you have with yourself. How do you influence yourself? Often people are very comfortable telling other people how to behave, but they're not as firm when it comes to themselves. They don't hold themselves accountable to their own commitments. They're too easy on themselves.

I started teaching the importance of self-esteem, self-confidence, and the unlocking of personal potential many years ago. I learned three wonderful insights. The first one was that *you become what you think about most of the time.*

For years, I fed my mind with positive, uplifting material, material on spiritual development. I spent thousands of hours reading books on spiritual development and personal motivation—all the great classics, such as works by Napoleon Hill and Norman Vincent Peale. Then I began to study metaphysics and how the mind and brain work in relation to the cosmos.

In 1981 I began teaching the law of attraction. It goes back 4,000 years before Christ, and it's been taught in the mystery schools over the generations. I studied it at great length and in great depth. I read books that had been written on it in the eighteenth and nineteenth centuries. I developed a deep understanding, and when I began to teach my two-day seminar on personal success, I included the law of attraction as one of thirty-two laws that I covered.

I also taught some sublaws of the law of attraction. There's a *principle of vibration*, which governs the entire universe. Every single form in the universe—water, glass, steel, uranium—is in a state of vibration and vibrates at a particular speed. Some vibrate very quickly, and some very slowly.

A related principle is the *law of sympathetic resonance*, also called *sympathetic vibration*. It says that if you have two pianos in a room, and you hit the key of C-flat on one piano and walk across to the other side of the room, that same string will be vibrating in the other piano. This is a very important principle in the universe.

Another concept is the *principle of repulsion*, whereby you can not only attract but repel things depending upon the emotion involved. In other words, if you have a negative emotion when you think about something, you can repel it from your life. If you have a positive emotion, you can attract it.

With sympathetic resonance, often you can walk into a room, look across it, and see a particular person. You'll introduce yourself to that person, and then be married for the rest of your life. The poet Kahlil Gibran said that this is how it happens: when you meet a person, either that will be the right person for you from the first moment of meeting, or it will never take place. That's why when couples are asked, "How did you meet?" both persons always remember the moment. They always remember that moment of sympathetic resonance.

There is a great deal of material available on the law of attraction now, but few people can make it work. Most of them don't understand that other elements are involved. One is faith. Faith has a powerful harmonic effect.

Another factor in attraction is the *principle of action*. As it says in the Bible, "Faith without works is dead." In other words, if you have a dream, a fantasy, or a goal but do not take actions consistent with that goal, it will just lie flat. It will have no effect. That's why so many people say, "I've been practicing the law of attraction for a year or two, and nothing happened." Why? It's because you went home and watched television instead of taking action.

Another principle is that *you become what you think about most of the time*, and you repel from your life the things that you discard.

There is also the principle of *negative versus positive emotions*. The only thing that stands between happiness and unhappiness is negative emotions. All negative emotions are learned, and being learned, they can be unlearned. You can almost detach a negative emotion, like a wire from a cable, so that it disappears. If you cancel out your negative emotions, all that's left are positive emotions. If you cancel out the negative emotions, and hook them up to positive poles, you create a force field of energy that draws into your life everything that you need to achieve your goal.

As we've already seen, negative emotions, such as a sense of failure and rejection, are imbued into children in the first three to five years by a constant flow of messages from their parents. If they receive a constant flow of positive messages, like healthy, nutritious food, they grow up happy, healthy, and self-confident.

The second thing I learned is that *you become what you teach*: the more you teach something, the more you internalize it yourself. If you really like the subject and teach it from your heart, you internalize it at deeper and deeper levels in yourself.

The third principle is that *you teach what you most need to learn*. For years, I've taught some subjects with tremendous enthusiasm, passion, and humor, and at a certain point I've moved on to other subjects. It's because I have internalized the subjects I taught; I don't need to learn them anymore. It's like teaching weight loss. At a certain point, you're slim, trim, and fit, and you eat good foods. You lose your enthusiasm to teach weight loss because you no longer need it anymore.

These concepts have enabled me to influence the lives of my children. I learned the principles, I practice them with my wife and my own children, and I began teaching them to other people. I have been really blessed in having been able to internalize these principles.

You can be positive most of the time by deciding to be. You can eliminate negative emotions by deciding to do so. You can develop an automatic response to negative situations and problems simply by pre-programming your mind to react in a positive way. The more you practice this, the more it becomes a part of the way you walk, talk, think, and act.

Over the last few years, I've had spinal stenosis, whereby your spine is almost like a corroded, rusted-out pipe that begins to corrode the wires of the nerves. They start to break down, and you start to have problems with the vertebrae. I've had six back operations. In addition, I had cancer, open heart surgery, and two torn rotator cuffs. Yet I've maintained a positive attitude.

I've lived a very busy, rough life for many years, I've traveled to 120 countries, and I've been through three or four wars. If you beat up your body when you're younger, it catches up with you when you're older. But through all of that, I've always remained relaxed and positive. I believe that I've been blessed, and I pass that belief on to my kids. My kids have never seen me other than positive. The worst that they've ever seen me is tired.

What has enabled me to maintain this attitude throughout all my difficulties? An attitude formed from reading spiritual and inspirational literature.

Brian Tracy's Three Insights for Unlocking Personal Potential:

1. You become what you think about most of the time.
2. You become what you teach.
3. You teach what you most need to learn.

6

The Sixth Quality: Preparation

The sixth characteristic of influential people is that *they are well prepared.* If they're going to make a presentation, they go through it many times. Preparation is everything. The most successful people in every field are thoroughly prepared. Every professional, whether it's a lawyer, a doctor, an architect, or an engineer, is well prepared when they have an important project.

Once I said to a professional, "I always overprepare."

"Brian," he said, "I don't believe there's such a word." I could see why he was one of the best-paid and most respected people in his field.

Brian Tracy's Guiding Principle of Preparation: *Even if you've prepared a hundred times, prepare one more time. Just one small detail may give you an edge.*

That's been my guiding principle: even if you've prepared a hundred times, prepare one more time. You never can tell. Just one small detail may give you an edge.

Even though communications have been moving faster and faster, they still require the human faculty—the ability to stand back, take a time-out, look at what is going on, analyze it, and discuss it with other people. Charlie Munger speaks about *deep thought*. It involves calling a time-out to think deeply and slowly about the information that has been conveyed.

My favorite word in this arena is *consequences*. In studying time management for more than thirty years, I've found that the potential consequences of a decision determine the value or importance of that decision.

Daniel Kahneman of Princeton University talks about fast thinking versus slow thinking—System 1 thinking and System 2 thinking. System 1 is fast thinking, like driving through traffic, making turns quickly, and avoiding other drivers. It's intuitive, it's experiential, it's fast, and it does not require a lot of depth. It's quite appropriate in traffic, because you don't have much time.

Daniel Kahneman's Two Types of Thinking:

1. *System 1 Thinking:* Fast thinking; intuitive and experiential—does not require a lot of depth; appropriate when the consequences are small and a decision can be quickly reversed.

2. *System 2 Thinking:* Slow thinking; every aspect of a situation must be deeply considered, like a good chess player; when the consequences of poor decision-making are quite serious.

You use System 2 thinking, slow thinking, when the consequences can be quite serious. The ramifications of a decision here—how many people it will affect and how long it will affect them—can be significant.

You use short-term thinking when there are limited consequences to your behavior: do you put one lump of sugar in your coffee, or two? But the car that you choose to buy, the course that you choose to study at university, the woman or man that you choose to marry, the job that you choose to take, the career path you choose to follow—these have enormous consequences. With decisions of this magnitude, you slow down so you can consider the ramifications, like a chess player. Kahneman points out that too many people use fast thinking in situations where they should use slow thinking.

One of the biggest mistakes is making a decision with too little thought. People don't consider all the possible ramifications. A good chess player sees where the game might go: If you do this, the competitor could do that. That would require that you do this, which means the competitor would do that. It goes back and forth in this way, so you have to be extremely thoughtful.

Slow thinking is required when the potential consequences can be enormous. Fast thinking is appropriate when the consequences are small and can be quickly reversed.

One of the most important recent advances in business is the use of AB thinking and rapid testing. You come up with an idea to change some part of your product or service. Then you take a test base, like 10,000 names (they call this *big data*, which now allows us to test very quickly). You send out two offers: an A offering, where you keep the pricing at the same level, to 5,000 names, and a B offering, where you raise or lower the price while adding a particular feature, to the other 5,000. Then you see what kind of response you get. If you have a positive response to the new feature from the B group—they respond positively and buy the new product because of the new benefit—that's a proven test case.

A wonderful rule says, "If you don't have data, then all you have is an opinion." Today you can get data very quickly. We have software in our business. Someone will come to us and say, "We have 200,000 or 300,000 names, and we want to do a joint venture with you. We want to sell your product to our names, and we'll split the profits."

We'll say, "OK, give us 5,000 or 10,000 names to test with." Then we will send these names a test offer of the product. We will very quickly know how many people respond, how much they buy, and what the difference is in comparison with previous offers. We'll also learn customers' purchasing patterns for other offerings, and this deep data will give us an enormous amount of information on our customers. We can determine, sometimes within an hour or two, whether or not this would be a good list, whether customers would buy this product in sufficient quantities at this price, and whether or not we should go ahead and make the same offer to the whole list of 200,000 names. We can test in the morning, and in the afternoon we can decide whether not or to send out the same offer to 200,000 people.

This process illustrates a rule for testing your business offerings: change one element of the offer and send it out to 5,000 people, and leave the other element of the offering unchanged and send it out to another 5,000.

Then look at your response rates. Do you get a substantial positive response rate with the new option? That can tell you to go in that direction. If you get a negative response rate, you can withdraw quickly.

The rule is test, test, test, and prove, prove, prove as fast as you can. Today companies might make two or three AB testings on the same product, with slight tweaks or changes in the offer, on the same day.

Entrepreneurs wonder how they can attract venture capital. A venture capitalist is very much like a banker, who is in the business of making good loans. A good loan is a loan that will be paid back with very high levels of consistency and dependability. Bankers' careers are determined by how often they make good loans and whether or not they make bad loans.

Whenever you talk to someone and you're asking for their money, the first thing that they're concerned about is getting their money back. They have no limit to the places where they can lend money, so that's not a concern to them.

You see advertisements on television where a woman comes into a banker's office. She puts her feet on the desk and says, "I've got a good credit rating; you can do better than the rate you're offering." She acts as if she owns the banker because of her credit rating and the banker has to acquiesce to give her a loan.

Whoever puts those ads together is preying on the ignorance of the public. In fact, the safest word that a banker can say is *no*: that completely prevents the possibility of loss. The same is true for venture capitalists. If they make a loan that is not paid back, or even paid back late, these nonperforming loans jeopardize their career. Each bank has managers at different levels, each of whom judged by how many performing loans they have approved and how many nonperforming loans they have on their books. A banker with too many or too big nonperforming loans is in great danger.

As we've seen in the news, there have been several cases where bankers have bankrupted their banks because they snuck around behind their bosses' backs. They made loans that did not comply with the financial requirements, although they personally thought that these would be a big score for the bank. Then they had to put in more and more money and hide the mistake more and more, and finally they ended up taking the banks down for several billion dollars—big international scandals. These are the most terrifying stories in banking.

In short, bankers want to make safe loans. Your job is to persuade them that this is a safe loan: if you lend this money to me, it's safe, it's a smart loan, and you can be absolutely guaranteed to get it back.

When I came to San Diego, I opened my first bank account, a corporate account, and I went to borrow

---

Brian Tracy's Rule for Entrepreneurs trying to secure
venture capital for their business: Take nothing for granted.
Provide the data and business plan required to convince
the banker that they are making a safe loan and
will easily get their money back.

---

money. My business had been in operation for five years, but it had been in Canada. I had assets, I had cash flow, I had enough money to lease offices and buy and lease furniture; I had a home, money, car, and bank account. Even so, I was treated like a penniless vagrant who had come in off the street asking for money.

Later I became good friends with the banker. I learned that bankers want $5 of collateral for every dollar they lend you, so you have to show that if they lend you $1, you have $5 somewhere to back it up. I had to prove that I had royalties coming from my audio programs. I had to sign those royalties over to the bank so that if there was any delay in payment, the audio company would be ordered to pay those royalties directly to the bank, not to me. I had a home, and I had to sign it over to them. At that time, you had to make a 20 percent deposit to get a mortgage, so I had, say, more than $100,000 in equity in my home, and I had to sign that over. This was all for a $50,000 loan.

I also had a business with customers and accounts receivable; I had money coming in. I had to sign that over. I had to sign over my car. I had to sign over a piece of property which I had bought with two other investors. I had to scrape together what was acceptable to them: $5 for every $1 that I wanted to borrow before they would lend me the money. I eventually did.

This is standard when you're starting off with a bank. For someone that has no credit history with the bank, it is standard that they require 5:1 leverage, 5:1 collateral.

One professor giving a lecture said that when you start your own business, you never invest your own money. You invest the bank's money. You keep your own money for your own reserves and your own expenses, and you don't spend a penny; you have the bank invest it. You prepare a financial statement that shows the bank that you will generate the sales and the revenue, and that will be all fine.

I still shake my head at that—and that professor was advising MBA students. If you went to a bank saying, "I'm not going to put any of my own money in it, but I expect you to put up 100 percent financing because of my sweet little business plan," they would laugh you out onto the street.

To raise money, you persuade lenders that you are a safe bet. Because of the money that you are generating, the money you've generated in the past, and your successful experience in other businesses, this is a safe loan.

Lenders look for an ability for an entrepreneur to hit their
numbers. It's just as bad for you to miss your numbers on
the downside as on the upside.

Once the entrepreneur has proven their performance
to the bank's satisfaction, it will lend them a little, and
then a little bit more. At length, the bank will start to
lend them serious money.

You have to crawl slowly before you crawl faster;
you walk slowly before you begin to walk faster. Finally,
you reach the point where you're successful, and you
make a lot of money. All your investors and your bankers are paid back. You open the champagne, and you do
your IPO.

At that point, the banks are open to helping you,
because you're a proven commodity. You have proven
that you can take other people's money, work with it, generate profits, and pay it all back. The bankers will line up
for a person who has been successful. They love to lend
to people who have proven that they can take money and
can grow it safely and dependably.

Lenders also look for an ability to hit your numbers. If you say that in your first year, you're going to
hit $100,000 in sales with $10,000 in profit, the second
year will be $250,000 in sales, and the third year will
be $500,000, the bankers will watch how closely you

hit your numbers. It is just as bad for you to miss your numbers on the downside as on the upside. Say you projected you would hit $100,000 in your first year, but you hit $200,000. This tells the banker that you really didn't understand your numbers or your business. You were not able to project properly. You didn't understand your market, your pricing, or your competition.

People think, "I broke the bank; I beat all the numbers." A financial supplier considers that a detriment, because it means that you don't know what you're doing financially.

Think carefully about your financial projections. Make sure they're accurate, and hit your projections. This will give you great influence on providers of finance. A person who has a record for hitting their numbers, being on time, and making the sales and profits is a person that's safe to lend to.

I worked with a man who could borrow $50 million with a telephone call. I watched him do it. He had put me in charge of a major business. I had done a complete financial prospectus for it and worked out how much we would need for eighteen months. He called the president of a major bank and said, "I need $50 million. I have all the numbers laid out here, and we'll send them over to you for your inspection. But I'll need about $50 million. After that, we can be looking at a business that's two or three times that size." The

---

**Preparation is essential for acquiring top-rate talent.
Do your homework on all new hires—including
extensive background checks.**

---

banker said, "All right, Charles, if you say it's a good number, then we'll approve it on the phone. Send over the papers."

Preparation is also essential for acquiring first-rate talent. Again, nothing replaces doing your homework—doing extensive background checks. Some of the biggest companies in the world have made enormous mistakes by not doing enough due diligence (my two favorite words in business).

People tend to overstate their accomplishments. My company does a lot of videos. We hire freelancers. They say they have been in charge of a particular production: they'd produced a video for a particular company. You'd check it out and find that in fact this person was a cameraman, or a sound man, on the shoot. They tell you they produced it when actually they were one of about twelve people on a crew. That's standard in the industry: people take full credit for anything they work on.

With regard to businesses, say the person claims to be in charge of building a multimillion-dollar division of a company. You call up the company and you ask, "What was the actual role of this person in this project?" You often find out that they were one of a large crew.

According to the big headhunters, 54 percent of all CVs are exaggerated; they're lies. When you interview a person and look over their CV, say, "I'm going to be talking to everybody whose name is on this list of recommendations. Is there anything that they might tell me that you might want to tell me in advance?" At that point, they'll start to give you the real truth.

Check and double-check. The rule is to check at least three people who have worked with a given person. Ask, "Whom did you work with, who was your boss, who were the key people that you worked with?" and call them separately. The person's coworkers could give tremendous insights.

Do due diligence. The only real predictor of future performance is past performance, so the only thing that you can depend on is the fact that a person has actually accomplished what they claim, and somebody else confirms their claims.

We talk about transferability of results. You hire a person because you believe that they have gotten results somewhere else that they can transfer to your situation,

"The only real predictor of future performance, is past performance. . . ." —Brian Tracy

and they will get the same results for you that they got for another organization. If you're being hired, you have to prove to them that you did get these results.

The above points highlight the absolute necessity of preparation in practically all areas, whether it's a matter of market research, lining up financing, or putting the right people to work in your business.

7

The Seventh Quality: Loving People

The seventh major component of influence is *loving people*.

How do you become charismatic? I've written a book called *The Power of Charisma*, coauthored with Ron Arden, who has directed 150 plays on the London stage. Ron and I talk about how you can become a warm and emotive person so people will like you, consider you charming, and be much more open to your influence.

The essential step is very simple: you become interested in other people. The process is much like sales:

Brian Tracy's Simple, Essential Step for Loving Others:
Become genuinely interested, even fascinated,
with other people.

---

you ask them questions about themselves, and you listen closely and attentively to the answers, as if whatever the person has said is fascinating.

If you want people to be fascinated by you, be fascinated by them. Use a series of extremely effective questions. You say, "Hello, my name is Brian Tracy. What's yours?"

The person says, "Dan."

"Really, Dan?" You repeat the person's name. "What sort of work do you do, Dan?"

"I work in recording."

"Holy smokes. What does that involve? What sort of work are you doing now in that area?" Another great question is, "How did you get into that area of work anyway?"

Then listen. Whatever the person says, just listen, listen, and listen until they stop talking. Then say, "What did you do next?"

In short, you use these three questions over and over:

1. What do you do?

2. How did you get into that line of work?

3. What did you do next?

The process is like getting three rings spinning. You keep asking these three questions. People love to talk about their career history. They will add another spin to the wheel; they will say, "I started this way. Now I'm working in this area, but it hasn't been working out, so I'm looking at something else."

Every so often people will pause, because they're not sure if you're interested or if you're just being polite. You immediately repeat the third question: "Then what did you do? What did you do after that?"

You can take the process further with questions like, "What would you advise someone who is thinking of going into your industry? What have been the greatest influences on you in getting into this industry? What did you do that had the greatest impact on your career?" Just keep asking people over and over about their careers.

After sixty minutes, you can say, "Thank you very much. I don't mean to keep you from other people, but you seem to have a fascinating life, and I hope I will get a chance to talk to you again."

"Yes, by all means." The other person will go away thinking, "That's the most charming man I ever spoke to." All you probably did was ask five questions over the course of an hour.

Later you can contact this individual and say, "You and I spoke the other day at so-and-so's social function.

Several questions to show genuine interest in other people:

1. What do you do?
2. How did you get into that line of work?
3. What did you do next?
4. What would you advise someone who's thinking of going into your industry?
5. What have been the greatest influences on you getting into this industry?
6. What did you do that had the greatest impact on your career?

I've got a friend who is interested in the same business that you're in. I was wondering if you might give him a little guidance, because he's not entirely sure about what to do." That person will open doors for you because instead of trying to impress them, you allowed yourself to be impressed by them.

In managing people, the starting point is to realize that everybody does things for their reasons, not yours. Whenever you present a new idea or piece of information, always do so as a way of improving the life or work of the other person. A person has to see a direct connection between what you're asking them to do and an improvement in their own conditions.

**People always act to improve themselves in some way.
Therefore, to be a more influential manager,
show others how to do a good job, and advance
to the next level in their career.**

Remember this basic psychological principle: people only act to improve themselves in some way. You show them that if they do this job well, they can improve their own situation. They can make a greater contribution, which will make them more valuable, which will make them more respected by others. This in turn will prove that they are capable of greater responsibility so they can earn more income.

Always think in terms of what people want. Point out to them how they will be better off, they will be more respected, they will get superior results, and they will advance if they do a good job.

Professional soldiers pray for peace but hope for war. They pray for peace because war is terrible and people are killed, but they hope for war because it provides military personnel with opportunities to advance quickly. They can perform in dangerous situations and win victories that will lead to rapid promotion. In wartime, you can be promoted faster in a few weeks or months than during your whole career in a peacetime army.

One way to influence people is to say that if you do a really good job here, it can open up doors for you. People want to get ahead, they want to advance, and opportunities to advance motivate them to do a better job.

I sit on two or three boards of directors, and because of my background in strategic planning, they will often ask me to conduct a strategic planning exercise for the organization. Before the meeting, I will speak to different board members who I know are influential. Rather than dropping a load of new ideas on them, I will go over the things that I'm planning to cover. I'll also talk about the consensus we would like to have by the end of the day and say that I really need their input. I will ask if they have any questions or suggestions for making the meeting successful. I'll also say, "You are highly respected by everyone on the board, so your contributions will be highly respected as well. I'd very much appreciate your help."

If you want more than one person in a meeting to come your way, talk to each of them in advance. Get them on board, tell them what you're trying to do and where you're trying to go, and get them to contribute their two cents' worth. It's quite amazing how helpful they will be for you.

If I'm leading the meeting and want to make it successful so that I achieve my objective and ensure that action is taken, I will open by explaining the big pic-

---

To be more influential when conducting a meeting, get agreement on a course of action, who is going to carry it out, and *when* and *how* you will measure the results.

---

ture: "Our job today is to make critical decisions in these particular areas." I also say, "This is my method: We don't want a democracy, where some vote for, some vote against, some are on board, and some are not on board. We want to reach a point where everybody here is so clear and satisfied that we have a consensus. That will require your best thinking and your best contributions. I want to elicit those contributions."

Here is a technique I use. I'll take a $100 bill, tack it up on a whiteboard, and say, "This $100 is for the first person who asks a dumb question or who makes a dumb comment in the course of our discussions today. And I can promise you one thing: nobody's going to get the $100, because there is no such thing as a dumb comment, a dumb question, or a dumb observation. Everything is wide open."

Then we go on, and everybody feels completely loose: what about this, and what about that? Why don't we do this, or why don't we do that? Have we ever thought of doing this, which is the opposite of what we're doing now? By the end of the day, everybody is contributing and sharing their best ideas.

If you're running a meeting, it's good to say, "We will end the day with a complete consensus. Everybody will agree with everybody else, and we'll all be happy with the conclusion."

Of course, you can reach consensus, but actually moving the goal forward is another matter. This is a common problem. You may reach consensus, leave, come back a week later, and find nothing has happened. It's often because a specific responsibility has not been assigned to a specific person, with a specific number and a specific deadline. You also have to say, "We'll agree on exactly what is to be done, who is to do it, and when it is to be done by, along with the measurement for completion."

If you get agreement on a course of action, who exactly is going to carry it out, and when and how will you measure the results? We go around the table, and each participant agrees to take on some part of the project, with a specific deadline and specific results. Everybody is crystal clear about their responsibilities. We write down the minutes, which we circulate so that everybody can see on paper what each person has committed to do, exactly when it's to be done, and how it will be measured.

There's a wonderful observation in business that says, if you want to be successful, measure everything. If you want to be rich, measure everything financially. The best thing you can do in discussing anything in business is to attach a financial number to each activity and then attach a financial number to each responsibility. This number will be used to measure whether or not we have achieved this goal.

I've already pointed out how every job is ultimately a sales job. Successful sales is closely bound up with influence. It is built around influencing others to make buying decisions that in their own best interests. As we saw in the previous chapter, people need to be able to sell their ideas to bankers and venture capitalists. You even need to sell your worldview to your children. How, then, are influence and success in the sales profession related?

In 1995, Daniel Goleman published a book that had a blockbuster impact, called *Emotional Intelligence*. He said that your emotional quotient (EQ) is more important than your intellectual IQ. Your EQ is your ability to interact effectively with others. According to Goleman, EQ—your ability to persuade, influence, negotiate, communicate, move people to do (or not do) certain things—accounts for 85 percent of your success.

The most successful people in every field are more influential than others. They have an impact on others:

According to Daniel Goleman, your *EQ*—
your ability to persuade, influence, negotiate,
communicate, and move people to do (or not do)
things—accounts for 85% of your success.

others listen to them and are moved by them to do or not do things.

I started selling from door to door when I was ten years old. I sold soap. Later on, I sold lawn mowing services, Christmas trees, and newspapers. Then I worked for several years as a laborer. I got back into sales when I was twenty-four, and again went out and knocked on doors. The whole sales training process at that time was, "Here's your cards; here's your brochures; there's the door." I used to joke that trying to sell without any training is the best weight-loss program in the country. I lost probably ten pounds when I started to sell, because I would work long hours knocking on doors, presenting my product, and not making sales.

I wasn't afraid to work, because up to that time I had been in laboring jobs—factories, mills, ships, and farms. I would go out and knock on doors all day. I probably knocked on sixty to seventy doors per day. In my first year in selling, I probably made 20,000 calls. I got rejected about 19,500 times, but I kept on knocking on doors.

Finally I began asking, why are some people more successful than others? I found that the process of selling is similar to the process of communication, or persuading or influencing anyone. When you knock on a door, you're meeting someone you've never met before in your life. Your goal is to go from that meeting to persuading them to give you money for your product. Selling is promising that your product or service is what you say it is and will do what you say it will do; you deliver on the promise later. In essence, people are giving you money for promises, and that's a hard sell. You're going around saying, "I've got promises. Who will give me money?" You're selling air, if you like.

After six months, I asked one of the top salespeople in my company, "Why are you much more successful than I am? Why are you selling ten times as much as anyone else?" He had loads of money; he was very successful.

"Show me your sales process, and I'll critique it for you," he said.

"I don't have a sales process. I just get in front of people and talk to them. I tell them about my product and service and how it works."

"No, that's not the way you do it. The first thing you do when you meet a new person is ask them questions. The more you ask questions and listen to the answers, the more they will like and trust you."

From that day on, I began studying sales. Instead of talking, I would ask questions. I would ask people about what they were doing in the area of my product. Was it working for them, what were their plans for the future, and what were their goals? If I could show them a better way to achieve their goals, would they be interested in looking at it?

As a result of asking these questions, my sales went up by a factor of ten within a year. I began to read everything I could find on selling. I listened to the first audio programs on the subject. I began taking sales seminars and workshops and listened to top people explain how they sold their products.

The process always began with an opening, an introduction, establishing rapport, asking questions so that the person liked you, and listening closely to the answers. Then it was a matter of finding out what the prospect was doing and what they needed. You went on to show the prospect how the product or service could help them achieve their goals and improve their lives at a reasonable price. Finally, you answered their questions or objections, closed the sale, and finally got resales, recommendations, and referrals.

An enormous amount of research has been done on the selling process. But there has also been research on the process that the customer goes through, starting with a cold call: meeting with the salesperson, never having seen them or thought about the product before. What cycle goes through their heads that leads them to say, "Here is my money"?

I began to study the subject from both sides, and I found that they fit together like two gears. If you sell the way the customer buys, you will increase your sales.

As Theodore Levitt of the Harvard Business School found, all sales are relationship sales, and all selling is

---

According to Tim Sanders, author of *The Likeability Factor*, even if a customer wants your product or service, they will not buy from you unless they like you, trust you, and feel that you are acting in their best interest.

---

relationship selling. Your success is determined by how much the prospective customer knows you, likes you, trusts you, feels comfortable with you, and is willing to buy from you.

A book came out in 2006 called *The Likeability Factor*, by Tim Sanders. It asked, on a scale of 1 to 10, how likable are you to your customers? That's going to determine exactly whether or not they will buy from you. Even if they want your product or service, they will not buy from you unless they like you, trust you, and feel that you are acting in their best interest.

In 2010, I went through a very difficult situation. I had invested a lot of money in a business, but it hadn't succeeded. I got a classical textbook throat cancer that comes from particular types of stress. I discussed this with an ayurvedic doctor in Malaysia, who said, "That comes from not being heard; you're feeling terrible frustration and anger because people are not listening to you. You're trying to convey a message to them, and they will not listen." Of course, these people would not, and did not, listen. They bankrupted the company and lost all my money.

If you allow other people to influence you by being open to *their* influence, they will become more and more open to *your* influence.

It reminded me of how important it is to feel that other people are listening to you. The more important people are in your life, the more important it is that they listen to you. The way to become more influential in your life is by making the members of your family, starting with your spouse, very important to you.

It's a perfect law of reciprocity. If you make it clear to other people that you really take their thoughts, feelings, and ideas into consideration, they will take *your* thoughts, feelings, and ideas into consideration. To the extent that you allow them to influence you and are open to their influence, they will become more and more open to your influence.

With my children, I say, "I will never force you to do anything, and I'll never forbid you from doing anything. Whatever you decide to do, I will support you 100 percent. I will give you my opinion about whether I agree or disagree, but I will never force you to do anything. You are always free to choose."

In our family life, whenever we would have an argument, I'd say, "I may argue or disagree with you, but if you have a good point of view and you can persuade me of it, I'll do what you want."

This was when the kids were five, six, and seven years old. They've always grown up knowing that if they can make their case, if they can give good reasons for doing or not doing something, their father will support them 100 percent.

It's made for a marvelous family experience. We've always supported our children, given them permission to do what they wanted, and allowed them to influence us if they came up with a good idea. Instead of shouting and screaming, they would reason the matter out and present their case like a lawyer in a courtroom. I would say, "From what you've said, I see that you are right and I'm wrong, so we'll do what you want." They were proud that at five or six years old, they could win their father over by presenting their arguments thoughtfully.

I've studied power and influence in business, and the quality of a relationship between the boss and the employees is largely determined by how much the employees feel that the boss is open to their influence. If the boss is fixed and inflexible, the morale of the organization will be low. People will say, "My opinion really doesn't matter or count. I've had an enormous amount of experience in this job, and my boss ignores that." However, when a person believes, "I can have a very strong influence on my boss; I can go to him and can present my point of view, and if he sees it, he will change his mind," morale will be high.

In my office, we have a lot of disagreements: not arguments but disagreements. If an employee wants to make a certain investment, I'll ask, "What is your reasoning? Why do you want to do that?"

The employee knows the question is coming and will explain: "This is why I think we should do this, or spend this amount of money."

I may say, "At this point I don't agree, and I will give my reasons."

"Yes, what you said is true, but there are two things that you hadn't considered."

When they've explained these points, I will say, "I hadn't thought about that, but you're right. Your conclusion is better than mine. We will do what you think is best."

There's a tremendous flexibility within our office. The boss is always open to being influenced by a good argument or a good set of reasons from someone else. I've always made it clear that if employees have a better argument, I will listen. I will abandon my position, even if I'm very adamant about it, if they turn out to have a better idea.

I have no ego involvement in being right. Once you've removed ego involvement, you eliminate most of your problems. I've studied this in detail in psychology and practiced it in my family life and my business life, and it works extremely well.

When I got married, I told my wife, Barbara, that I would give her 51 percent of the vote in all issues that affected the family and the children, and I would have 51 percent of the vote with regard to work and business. It's the best decision I ever made. With family issues, I will argue my 49 percent, but in the final analysis she decides.

She's always been right. I will disagree occasionally. "Yes," she says, "but you don't understand." Sometimes she'll say, "Intuitively I think this is the best way to go. I don't have a logical reason for it. I don't disagree with you for wanting to go in a different direction, but I feel that this is what we should do, and I have 51 percent of the vote." It's made our relationship smooth for nearly forty years.

Of course, every couple has its own rules. Nobody can predict or set down rules for any other couple, because human beings are so different from one another. In a couple, you have two complicated chemical beings mixed together to form an extraordinarily complicated unit, so I never pass judgment on anyone else.

I do say that the most important thing is to listen to your intuition and follow where it leads you. My philosophy was formed very early. I began to study the qualities

---

The most important quality of a good marriage relationship and a good parent-child relationship is *respect*.

---

of a good marriage and being a good parent, and I found that respect is more important than anything else. As long as you have respect, you can have all kinds of disputes and disagreements, and it will work out. But if the respect ever goes, everything else goes very quickly. So I have never violated that respect. I've always respected my wife and our children. Today they respect their spouses. Their relationships are solid and positive, because they have seen the way I've treated Barbara and the way she's treated me. That's how they expected to be treated when they found spouses, and that's how they treat each other. As a parent, you are a role model for your children. You set a standard that they seek to repeat when they become adults.

Sometimes, of course, you may have to influence your children in a certain direction. In order to retain or increase your influence, you have to have an ongoing relationship of openness, honesty, and respect, so there's never any buildup, there's never any negativity, there's never any gunnysacking—storing up grievances. Each person is perfectly honest with the other person all the time. We deal with any negative concerns as they come up.

When I was very young, I read that if you're married to the right person, your spouse should be your best friend. When you meet the right person for you, you recognize that you've met your best friend; this is a dream relationship. If this person is your best friend, there's nothing that you would not share with them, nothing you would not tell them, nothing that you would hold back from them.

That's what happened with Barbara and me. When we met, we became best friends from the beginning, and we've been through four children, five grandchildren, and lots of life, but we've never had any real problems at all.

At times, you may have a close friend who is drinking too much or has been overtaken by cynicism or anger. People often wonder how to influence others in these cases.

As a matter of fact, people don't change. Or rather, they do change, but only under certain circumstances. As Peter Drucker said, it is not that miracles don't happen, it's that you cannot depend upon them.

Often we become frustrated because we're unhappy with something that another person is doing, and we urge them to change. By doing this, we can trigger the

---

"It's not that miracles don't happen, it's that you can't depend on them." —Peter Drucker

---

greatest fear—of rejection or disapproval. Whenever you suggest that the person is not acceptable in their current form, you're triggering this fear of rejection. The worst of all fears is summarized in the words "I'm not good enough." In many ways, they feel they're not good enough in terms of school, physical fitness, sports, work, sales, or providing for their families. Most people wrestle with this issue all their lives.

Your job is never to trigger the feeling "I'm not good enough, I'm somehow inferior." People may change, but only if they really desire to change, only if they have a personal wake-up call and firmly decide that they are going to do something different.

I have a good friend who was extremely obese. He looked as if he was trying to smuggle a bag of potatoes out of a store and his suits were made to cover the bag.

I saw him recently, and he's lean and trim. About a year before, he had decided to take the weight off, so he became a strict vegan and lost 130 or 140 pounds. He looked as if his neck was atop a tent, because his clothes hadn't been retailored for him yet. He had been over-weight for two or three decades, and he finally decided to change.

I have met other people who have made decisions to stop smoking, stop drinking alcohol, stop eating sugar, or become strict vegans. But only they can make those decisions.

If you try to tell a person that they should change something, you're essentially saying, "You're not good enough as you are. I don't approve of you as you are. As you are, you are inferior to me." This causes anger, feelings of inferiority, and frustration.

That's why the greatest gift that you can give a child is unconditional acceptance: you never criticize the children. You just accept them 100 percent, unconditionally, for who they are, for good or bad.

8

The Eighth Quality: Communication

The eighth quality of influential people is that they are *great communicators*. Peter Drucker said that there are three tools of the executive: One is the one-on-one conversation. The second is two- or three-person conversation. The third is the presentation.

A major part of effective communication is the skill of public speaking. One of the smartest things you can do is join Toastmasters or a similar speakers' association. They will teach you how to speak on your feet, how to stand up and communicate with others, how to open conversations, and how to win friends and influence people. As you become a more confident speaker, you'll get opportunities to speak for other groups. In time, you'll be known as a person who's quite confident speaking on their feet. You will be introduced to people who will open doors for you. You will be invited to clubs and associations. You'll have more social opportunities with people who will hire you, promote you, and recommend you to others.

You can read books on communication. I've already mentioned Robert Cialdini's *Influence*. You can read books by Dale Carnegie, Earl Nightingale, and other great communicators. You can listen to audio programs by famous communicators and learn how to open a conversation and be funny, interesting, and persuasive.

Elbert Hubbard (1856–1915) was one of the greatest writers in American history. He was so prolific that he built his own publishing company. People would ask him, "Mr. Hubbard, how do I become a successful writer like you?" He said, "The only way to learn to write is to write and write." He also said, "The only way to learn to become a good speaker is to speak and speak."

Communication skills are all learnable, but you cannot become a great communicator sitting at home watching television. You have to get out and speak, you have to join associations and organizations, and you have to go to their meetings on a regular basis. You have

---

"The only way to learn to write, is to write and write.
The only way to learn to become a good speaker,
is to speak and speak." —Elbert Hubbard

---

to introduce yourself to people, talk to them, stand up, make comments, and become known as a communicator. That will open more doors for you. When you speak well, people will think you're more intelligent than you may actually be.

Over the past forty years, we've gone from landline phones, mimeograph machines, typed letters, in-person meetings, and longer attention spans to smartphones, digital files, emails, texts, Zoom meetings, and shorter attention spans.

The purpose of all this technology is to help us achieve our goals, especially in communication, faster and more easily. Every advancement in human history has resulted from an attempt to communicate faster, more easily, more economically, and with greater clarity to a greater number of people.

In fact, the purpose of language is to communicate. Words are condensed thoughts, so a word like *love* or *hope* or *understanding* can have many meanings. The *Oxford English Dictionary* lists fifty-four meanings for the word *nice*, each of which is correct in the proper context.

Good communication is a message that is fully received
and understood by the listener. If the thought is
received, but the person misses a critical element
that is called *noise*, not communication.

When you combine such a word with another one
that has twenty or thirty meanings, you can put together
very complex thoughts. The complex thought of one person combining two words and the complex thought of
another who is attempting to understand them can be
completely different. Today many of the most ancient
texts, including the Bible, have been so misinterpreted
that they have little connection to what the original writers were saying.

Sometimes one word, even one comma, in a legal
contract can invalidate it. I was reading about a legal
dispute that took place in Chicago a few years ago. The
judge concluded that the location of a single comma
changed the meaning of a clause so significantly that he
awarded $40 million to the plaintiff. If the other person
complained or appealed against his judgment, then it
would go up to $100 million.

Communication can also be hampered by thoughts.
You say something to me, but as you're saying it, another
thought breaks through my mind. I receive your thought,
but I've missed a critical element. This is called *noise*.

One of the words that you used is different from the word that I received, and so I use another word to repeat the idea in order to make sure that I've got it clear. You say, "No, that isn't exactly what I meant; what I actually meant to say was *this*."

Look at how many misunderstandings can take place in a simple conversation. As a result, in the digital age, one of the most important things we can do is slow down, double-check, and corroborate.

When I was running my business, I would ask someone to do something, and he would say, "Yes, I will do this."

I would say, "Now repeat back to me what I just asked you to do."

"You just asked me to do this in this way by this time."

"No, that is not what I asked. I asked you to do *that* in *that* way by this time."

I developed the habit of having people bring a notebook, and as we talked, they would write down what I was asking them to do. Then I would say, "Now read it back." In 50 percent of cases, a simple conversation would be misinterpreted: the other person got a different message from the one I had intended. It would have led to a completely different course of action, which would have led to a completely different outcome.

During the Civil War, some have said that the high-water mark of the Confederacy was the Battle of Gettysburg in 1863. The Southern forces invaded the

North, and the two armies met unexpectedly at Gettysburg, Pennsylvania. The Southern troops were coming from the north and the Northern troops were coming from the south, and they met accidentally at this place. The battle began without anybody planning for it. It started moving without the generals in command knowing what was happening: the forces began coming from different places to join with each other.

The battle took place over three days. One of the most crucial moments was the second day, when the Confederate commander, Robert E. Lee, ordered General James Longstreet to take a position on the right flank of the Union forces, and to advance on the enemy position when the time was fortuitous. Longstreet did not believe that this was the best place to attack, so he moved his army forward about halfway and kept it there all day. If he had moved forward and kept pressing, he could have overwhelmed the Union forces, because they had not come up yet. The South would have won the Battle of Gettysburg.

Lee moved his troops forward, but Longstreet held his troops waiting in position for the entire day. It was only at four o'clock in the afternoon that Lee sent a message to Longstreet saying, "Why have you not moved your forces forward?"

Longstreet replied, "I thought you told me to move my forces forward when I felt it was fortuitous."

Lee replied, "Yes, but it's been fortuitous. Please move your forces forward now."

Longstreet didn't really want to, but he moved the forces forward. Unfortunately for him, by this time the federal troops were ready. They had come up overnight, and there were thousands of them, locked in along what was called Cemetery Ridge, and they had superiority on higher ground. There was tremendous fighting, and the Southern forces were pushed back. The second day ended in a stalemate. If Longstreet had moved forward on the second day, as Lee believed he had ordered him to do, he would have won, and the whole outcome of the Civil War may have been different.

Finally, on the third day, it was clear that the North had completely fortified Cemetery Ridge and the high ground. Lee ordered his last army, which was commanded by General George T. Pickett, to attack the center and break through. Pickett's Charge was organized: nine infantry brigades went forward, but this time it was too late. Pickett's brigades were beaten back. The Southern army was defeated and had to withdraw back to Virginia.

That was the high-water mark of the Confederacy. It never again achieved that level of power concentrated at a critical place. As a result, although it took almost two more years, the South lost the war.

Any one word, interpreted incorrectly, could lead to the collapse of a merger, a wrong decision in business, a wrong action by the customer.

All this occurred because of a misinterpretation of a word and whether or not a person had the discretion to move forward now or later.

Look at the billions of words generated every day on the Internet and on email. Any one of these, interpreted incorrectly or differently from what the speaker meant, could lead to the collapse of a merger, a wrong decision in business, a wrong action by the customer. It could even lead to the collapse of a company or the decline of an industry.

In short, you need to make sure not only that you communicate your message clearly, but that the person to whom you are communicating it understands it just as clearly.

9

The Ninth Quality:
Good Manners

The ninth quality of influential people is that they are *well-mannered*. Being well-mannered opens every door for you. The best families in all cultures bring up their children with strict manners. Children fight against these strictures when they're young. But because manners are integral to culture, when you get older, you will be attracted to men and women with the same cultural background as yours, who eat and behave correctly.

I remember going out with a girl when I was a teenager. Her parents put her through a one-year course on manners when she was sixteen. They taught these young

---

"I have traveled in eighty countries, and I have found that
if you can just learn *hello, how are you?, please* and *thank
you*, you can get halfway across any country in the world."
—Brian Tracy

---

ladies—and many young men as well—about how to set
a table, how to prepare a dinner, how to serve coffee and
tea, and how to greet people when they came in. Once
they learn these manners, they have them for life. From
then on, they only associate with people who behave the
same way.

It's very important that parents make sure that their
kids grow up with manners and are always polite, saying
please and *thank you.* I have traveled in eighty countries,
and I've found that if you can just learn *hello, how are
you?, please,* and *thank you,* you can get halfway across
any country in the world.

You can get that information from the first person at
the airport, or you can get a phrase book and learn those
words; that's all you really need. *Please* and *thank you*
are marvelous words. If you use them, everywhere in the
world people will open doors for you.

Another element of good manners has to do with
conversations. If somebody's talking to you and you're
only pretending to listen, that's not an act of integrity;
that's dishonesty. One of the worst things that can hap-

pen is that people can say something to you that you're not catching. You catch a half-message, you reach a half-conclusion, and you decide to do something that is incorrect. In addition to all else, good manners require listening patiently, totally, 100 percent, to the other person.

One great weakness of our society is that people are becoming distracted by electronic interruptions. Every time you allow yourself to be interrupted electronically, it takes you eighteen minutes to get back to work.

Your most valuable asset is your earning ability—your ability to do work that people will pay you for. Remember, all success in work life comes from completing tasks. If you leave your electronic interruptions on, you can never complete a task, and if you never complete a task, you can never be promoted.

Success is based on project completion. Projects have a beginning, a middle, and an end. They are finished and passed up or down the line. Electronic interruptions prevent you from accomplishing your projects and can increase the amount of time it takes to do a job by 500 percent. Instead of taking 100 minutes, it will take you 500 minutes, because you keep going away and coming back.

Today you see people walking on the street with their earphones, texting. They're walking into posts and knocking themselves out, or they're walking into traffic and getting hit by cars. Honolulu and other cities have passed distracted walking laws, which forbid pedestrians from walking while texting on their smartphones.

Each time you are distracted, your brain receives a jolt of dopamine, just like when you hear a bell ringing. According to a recent study, listening to your smartphone or accessing email is like standing by a slot machine in a casino. When the machine goes off, it rings. When your phone rings, it triggers the same response: "What did I win?" Intermittent reinforcement leads to you think, "Maybe it's a friend or relative; maybe it's a joke from one of my friends."

If you're talking to someone, and the phone rings, you immediately stop, turn away, and check your phone. A jolt of dopamine goes through your brain: you think, "I won something."

People are going through their whole day with their gadgets ringing. I suggest a new approach to electronic interruptions. First, don't check your email before 11:00 a.m. Second, once you check your email, turn it off and leave it off. Check it again at 3:00 or 4:00. Some people say to check it three times a day, at 10:00, at 1:00, and at 4:00. Then turn your device off, and leave it off. Don't even have it in the room.

When you go into a meeting of any kind, don't bring your electronic interruptions. Leave them outside or at your desk. Most people aren't taking notes in meetings.

They're totally focused on messaging. You cannot think two thoughts at the same time, so if you're distracted by the message, you cannot think about what's taking place in the meeting.

If you're talking with somebody in a one-on-one meeting, there's nothing more insulting than to sit there returning messages while the other person is talking. You don't remember anything they said, you're not paying attention to the message that comes in, and it's a complete waste of time.

Develop email etiquette: turn your devices off, and leave them off. Check them two or three times a day at

---

Tips for Managing Electronic Interruptions

1. Don't check e-mail before 11AM. Do important work first.

2. Once you are through checking your e-mail, turn it off.

3. Check e-mail again, only one, maximum two times more per day (at 1PM and 3PM).

4. Don't bring your phone or computer into a meeting; leave them outside at your desk.

5. If you must have your phone, leave it on "silent" so it doesn't distract you from the task at hand.

most; otherwise, leave them off. At the very least, leave them on silent so that they don't distract you from your work.

Many people's careers are being sabotaged by an addiction to the ring. They leave the device on, because the little hit of dopamine gives them a jolt, and dopamine is the same drug that is in cocaine. People get little cocainelike jolts every time they hear a bell, and soon they can't stop. You can stop in the morning for as long as you don't turn the device on. But as soon as you turn it on and you get the first ring, you're off to the races; for the rest of the day you're trapped.

Closely related to good manners are image and appearance. A client of mine told me about an extremely well-known person whom his company had brought in to speak. This man was very arrogant. He wore jeans, a T-shirt, and tennis shoes to speak to an audience of 800 business owners. He was very brash, and he threw his ideas around as if he was a great genius and these people were average. He made no effort to impress them. He sat on a stool casually, as if he was at a cheap bar, waving his arms, and talking about how smart he was and how much experience he had. He was twenty-nine years old, although the average age of the businesspeople in the audience was probably forty-five to fifty.

It was extremely incongruous. This man made no effort at all to dress or speak like a businessperson or to treat the audience like high-caliber businesspeople, which they were.

My client told me, "The difference between him and you is night and day. You look great, as if you've come out of a fashion catalogue. When you stand up to speak, people are convinced that you know what you're talking about."

During the 1990s and the 2000s, when there was a high-tech boom, people were going to work in their undershirts and making millions of dollars. Other people began to think, "Even though I'm not successful, I can dress like a bum too." They didn't realize that the people who dressed like bums were already successful: they had raised millions of dollars in venture capital and had Mercedes-Benzes in the parking lots downstairs. Most people have not earned the right to dress casually, because they've not succeeded at anything. They're not respected by anybody, including their peers.

Companies let employees dress poorly on two conditions. Number one is that they stay in the back office, because they have no future in the front office. The company doesn't want these employees meeting their customers. In the second place, the company gives the employees this leeway instead of salary increases. Rather than pay them more money, they allow them to dress down on Casual Friday.

> "If you want to be successful, dress the way
> successful people dress." —Brian Tracy

In Silicon Valley, people come to work dressed casually, but they have suits and ties in a changing room. Whenever bankers and e-venture capitalists visit, these workers change into suits and ties to meet with them. After they're gone, these people can go back to wearing crummy clothes.

If you want to be successful, dress the way successful people dress. Look in business magazines like *Forbes*, *Fortune*, and *Business Week*, and dress like the top executives you see there; dress like you're one of them. This will attract people to you. If you look like a successful person, they'll want to be around you. Remember, everything that you do either helps or hurts. Everything either adds to your credibility or takes away from it.

Here is an instance of how image and appearance can work for you. Once a young man decided he wanted to be successful in business. His father subscribed to the major business publications. When the man was a teenager, he began to read these publications, and he cut out pictures and biographies of business leaders. While other kids were collecting baseball cards and pictures of pop singers, he put together images of major executives. He would read the papers, and he'd cut out excerpts about their accomplishments. He fed his mind with pictures of successful businesspeople. He read about their backgrounds and interests, how they played golf and tennis. He made them his icons.

From the time he was a teenager, this young man was focused on getting into the boardroom. He began to imagine himself as one of these people and pattern himself after them. When he graduated from college, he got a job with a Fortune 500 company. Although it was at a very low level, he had been researching these companies, so he knew a lot about this one. He was attracted to the senior executives, who mentored him. By the time he was thirty-five, he had jumped twenty years in his career. He was a senior vice-president for a Fortune 500 company and was highly respected among his peers. He dressed, groomed, and carried himself professionally, and he had read all the articles and books about how to be more respected and influential. By the time he was forty, he was the president of a Fortune 500 company. He said the critical thing was that he patterned himself after influential people: "I looked at what they did, I looked at their lifestyle, I looked at their dress and their clothes."

When I started off selling investments at the age of twenty-four or twenty-five, I was taken aside by an older man, who said, "Brian, are you open to a little bit of advice on your dress?" I had come from a poor background, and I had a cheap suit.

This man walked me through the details of wardrobe. I threw away the few clothes that I had. He took me to a custom tailor, who made a properly fitting suit for me. It easily cost three or four times as much as an ordinary suit, but it looked beautiful. Then he had shirts made for me that fitted the suit, and then got ties that fitted the suit and the shirts.

By the time I was finished, I looked like a successful person. I was still calling on the same people, making presentations for financial plans and mutual funds, but my sales over the next couple of years went up ten times. These people introduced me to their friends and clients, and they opened doors for me. They could be proud to introduce me to someone, because I looked good.

I looked around at other people, both younger and older than I was, who looked poor. Sometimes they forgot to shave; sometimes their shoes looked as if a car had run over them. Their clothes didn't match properly, their ties were the wrong length relative to their shirts and jackets, and their suits were bought out of thrift shops.

Bit by bit I moved up. Dress was not the only thing that helped me, but it did encourage people to treat me differently. They opened doors for me, invited me to lunch at their clubs, and offered me positions. Looking good had a profound effect on my life.

People don't realize that 95 percent of the first impression that you make is the result of how you look

---

**95% of the first impression that you make,
is the result of how you look on the outside.**

---

on the outside. You might say, "They shouldn't judge me by the way I look on the outside," but *you* decide how you look on the outside. You choose your clothing and grooming in order to make a statement to the world: "Here I am. This is who I am. Take me or leave me, but this is what you get. What you see is what you get." *You* make that choice. If you choose to look poor, you cannot fault people who judge you by the way that you have asked them to judge you.

Furthermore, you yourself judge everybody else by the way they look. You may say, "Oh, no, I'm quite neutral. I get to know their personality and character." No, you don't, because you don't have time. In most cases, we judge people within five seconds. First impressions are lasting. When you're out calling on people, you cannot afford to make a bad first impression. You cannot afford to have them dismiss you.

10

The Tenth Quality: Perseverance

The tenth characteristic of influential people is that they *persevere in the face of difficulty*. Persistence and perseverance are the most important qualities for success, because you will have problems in life; the only question is how you respond to them.

In my twenties, I came across a body of psychological and metaphysical research that told me something that never left me. It informed me that it's possible to preprogram yourself mentally so that you can decide to persevere, no matter what goes wrong. You decide in

---

"It's not how far you fall, but how high you bounce
that counts." —Charlie "Tremendous" Jones

---

advance: "No matter what happens, I won't ever give up,"
and from then on you never will.

As my friend Charlie Jones used to say, "It's not how
far you fall, but how high you bounce that counts." Say,
"When I have a setback or difficulty, no matter what it
is, I will always respond in a positive way. I will bounce
rather than break."

People give up because they have not decided *not* to
give up. As my four children were growing, I would tell
them, "Something I know about you is that you never
give up."

They'd say, "How do you know? What if I have lots of
problems?"

"Yes, you may think that, but it's not true. You never
give up. You're not the kind of person that gives up."

Today all four are grown, and they never give up. It
never occurs to them to give up. It's like a part of their
genetics: they never quit at anything, and they're always
positive.

You can decide for yourself, "I never give up," and
from this day forward you never will. Say, "I never give
up. I never quit. I'm always positive. I always respond in
a positive way. I'm always prepared before I go into any-

thing." Say it to yourself even once, and your subconscious mind accepts it as a command: it becomes an operating principle of your life.

When I studied economics, psychology, and philosophy, I found that a great weakness of the human being is what I call the *E factor*, the expediency factor. People seek the fastest and easiest way to get what they want, with little concern for long-term consequences.

The *E-Factor* (The *Expediency* Factor) means people often seek the fastest and easiest way to get what they want, with little concern for long-term consequences.

Some people believe that the way to become successful is to find a trick. Once I was doing a coaching program in San Francisco with about ten or twelve people. Two or three of them were serious and were looking at building long-term businesses. The rest were semiserious, and they were talking about the tricks they were working on.

One woman was telling me about her website. She was going to develop an app and become a multimillionaire. I said, "Really? what's it going to do?"

"It's going to show women how they can get better resources and combine them together to get better jobs, and then check out the jobs to see if they're right for them."

"It sounds pretty complicated."

"Oh, yes, but you just hire a couple of engineers and tell them what you want them to do, and they do it."

"How do you pay these people?"

"You give them all a piece of the game."

"How is it going?"

"It's not going that well yet; I'm just getting going. I just got the idea now, but I expect to have it up and running and making a few million dollars a year by next year."

"Really?"

"Oh, yes, you just throw together the app and put it up. There are so many phones out there, it shouldn't be any problem at all."

"You know, a lot of other people are trying to develop apps as well."

"Oh, yes, but my idea is vastly superior to theirs. There are so many women out there that as soon as this is finished, half the female population will buy it."

"Why?"

"Because everybody wants to get better information about their jobs and their careers."

I let the subject go, because I thought she was living in cloud-cuckoo-land, and of course it turned out that she was.

Today there are more than a million entrepreneurs who are living at home, working alone or with their friends, to develop the next killer app. This number compares with that of farmers. There are more people working at home, thinking that they're going to develop a killer app and become rich, than there are farmers farming all the farms in the United States.

In fact it takes about seven to ten years of hard work for an entrepreneur starting in a new business to become a millionaire for the first time. The average for all self-made millionaires is about twenty-two years. These are people who work and work year after year. After twenty-two years, their accountant tells them, "By the way, you have a net worth of a million dollars." These people run mom-and-pop shops, coffee shops, garages, and similar businesses.

A related characteristic of successful entrepreneurs is hard work. Every one of them will say they were willing to work much harder than their peers. They started earlier, they worked harder, they stayed later. You've heard the old saying, "The harder I work, the luckier I get." I've spoken to countless self-made millionaires, and they'll tell you about their early experiences. They worked longer hours than anyone else: sixty hours a week or more. Often they would work for years before they managed to strike lightning.

Some entrepreneurs who put their heads down and work themselves silly can hit their target in about seven years. That's fourteen to sixteen hours a day, sixty to sev-

---

According to studies, it takes about 10,000 hours of hard work before you're producing a product or service at such a high level of quality that you're worth a million dollars.

---

enty hours a week, six to seven days a week, for seven years. According to the studies, it takes about 10,000 hours of hard work before you're producing a product or service at such a high level of quality that you're worth a million dollars.

The average self-made billionaire has worked about fifteen years—fifteen hard, solid years. They've all failed over and over again, failed, tried again, failed, tried again. After about fifteen years, they've had enough experience to get the right combination of people, influences, ideas, technology, opportunities, money, and reputation, and suddenly lightning strikes.

People offer seminars and online packages on how to get rich quick, how to make easy money, and how to use a special trick that they will generously teach you for several thousand dollars. If you follow their tricks, you'll get in and you'll get out, and make a whole pot of money.

That simply doesn't work. Remember, only about a fraction of 1 percent of people are going to become wealthy in the best of times. Even though we have computers that enable us to trade at breakneck speed, the competition is fierce. If you want to go into the financial markets, you're competing with some of the smartest and most aggressive people in the world, who are watching you to see if you have any insight that they can use to make an extra penny.

An enormous number of suckers are looking for easy ways to make money. They are the fair prey of others who are trying to sell them get-rich-quick programs. But most of the people selling these programs go broke when the market goes down. Many of them are broke already. Many of them have no money except for what they get from selling their programs. They're making money by talking you into buying their recommendations, but they're not making any money on actual investments.

I have a good friend who's a smart and wealthy businessman. People frequently ask him, "Would you invest in my great scheme, my product, my algorithm, my system?"

"Sure," he says. "I'll tell you what I'll do: I will show you all my financial results and how much I'm worth, if you will show me all your financial results and how much you're worth. If, as a result of working your system, you

---

Forget "get rich quick" schemes. Focus on working hard in your career, doing high-quality work and delivering a high-quality product; that's what will determine 90% of your success.

---

are doing better than me, then I'll invest with you. Otherwise we will part company, and we will not speak again. So show me how much money you have."

That's the end of every conversation. The person looks at the floor, says, "I don't think this is a good time for us to talk, so I'll go now," and gets up and leaves.

I was talking to another friend of mine, who owned and ran two restaurants that were full all the time. I asked him, "Mitch, what's the secret to having a successful restaurant?"

"It's very simple. Put it on the plate."

"How do you mean?"

"You can have all the decor, the lights, the mahogany, the music, and the staff, but the bottom line is, put it on the plate. It's what people are served; what it looks like and tastes like is more important than anything else."

Similarly, if you want to be a successful professional speaker, put it on the stage. The best advertisement for yourself is to give excellent talks which impress people. If you can do that, they'll hire you again and again.

Ninety percent of business success is based on the quality of the product as perceived by the customer compared to that of the competitor. The most successful companies have the highest-quality products, and the second most successful, the second highest-quality, and so on. The third and fourth—nobody even knows their names.

**How can you tell if you are good at your work?
You get regular job offers. That's the way the market
tells you that you're doing a first-class job.**

If you're a business owner, concentrate on offering a high-quality product. If you're an individual, 90 percent of your success will be determined by the quality of your work. If you do first-rate work, the news will get out everywhere. People will seek you out.

How can you tell if a company is selling a popular product? The answer is, a lot of people are coming to the store, as with Krispy Kreme doughnuts. When the Krispy Kreme trend was at its peak, people were lined up down the street to buy those doughnuts. People would buy them by the dozen, they'd sit out there on the curb or the tables, and they'd eat them right there, because the doughnuts tasted so good.

How can you tell if a restaurant is good? It's full. How can you tell if a store is good? It's full. How can you tell if you are good at your work? Here's the answer: you get regular job offers. People are always offering you a better job, and they offer to pay you more money if you go and work for them.

How many job offers have you had this month? How many people have approached you privately or publicly, called your home or office, taken you out for coffee or lunch, and offered you a job that will pay you more money? That's the way the market tells you that you're doing a first-class job, because everybody knows who does the best job.

I've worked with people who start businesses. The first question they'll ask is, "What's the best company in this industry?"

Someone will say, "ABC company."

"Great. Who's the best person over there?" They'll find out who's the best salesperson, the best manager, the best accountant. Then they'll say, "Set up an appointment with me. I want to talk to that person."

I had a friend who did this all the time. He would ask prospective employees, "How much do they pay you over there?"

"I don't know if I can tell you that."

"It's OK. It's confidential. Just tell me how much they pay you to do your job over there."

"I get paid $110,000 a year."

"I'll tell you what: I'll pay you 50 percent more if you come to do the same job for me." If the job was to be the president of the company, he would say, "I'll pay you double."

The other person says, "Gee, that's a lot of money."

Now the prospect's mind starts to dance with sugarplums and fairies. What could you do if you had double the income? Double the size of your house; put your kids in private schools; take vacations to Paris; buy your wife St. John knits; get yourself beautiful, tailored clothes; get new furniture and a new pool out in the back; join a golf club. Think of all the things you could do if you were earning twice as much.

A friend of mine said, "All right, I'll take your offer. But how are you going to pay me twice as much? According to your financial statements, the company is getting by, but you don't have that much money."

"You're going to figure it out. You're the president. You're running the company. You're going to figure out where you're going to get the extra sales and profitability so that you can pay yourself. Can you do that? If you can't do that, I'm talking to the wrong person."

This entrepreneur bought several companies, and this was his standard strategy. When a prospect asked him, "How are you going to get the money to pay me?" he would say, "You're going to get it for me. You're going to increase sales and profits so we can afford to pay you twice as much." These people almost invariably ended up meeting that goal.

Afterword

Many people think influence is a matter of knowing the right people, being in the right place at the right time, or coming from the right background.

These can be major factors in influence, but as we've seen, throughout this book, other things are far more important.

Being and seeming are not identical, but they are closely related, and success is not possible until they match. To achieve a high level of influence, you have to have strong internal qualities: you set and achieve goals, you're sincere and well-informed, and you have the highest standard of integrity. You live in truth with yourself, tell the truth to yourself, and live in truth with other people.

Your external characteristics need to correspond to what you are inside: you have to be friendly, well-mannered, well-dressed, a good communicator, and a people lover. Pull all of these elements together into one dynamic package, and you're guaranteed to be extremely influential. You can go out into the world, interact with many different types of people, and get their help in achieving all of your goals.

Make sure to always use your influence for the good.

Printed in the USA
CPSIA information can be obtained
at www.ICGtesting.com
JSHW012033140824
68134JS00033B/3032